Social Media Marketing 2019

The Must-Know Practical Tips and Strategies for Growing Your Brand, Becoming an Influencer and Advertising Your Business Using Facebook, YouTube, Twitter and Instagram

By Gary Clyne

Table of Contents

Introduction _____ 5

Social Media Marketing – The New Era of
Brand Promoting _____ 7

Your Best Strategy for Marketing on Social
Media _____ 12

Prioritizing the Top Platform for Your
Brand _____ 20

Marketing on Facebook _____ 27

   Think Like a Follower _____ 27

   Boosting Your Facebook Page _____ 30

   Your Strategy for Encouraging
   Engagement _____ 38

   Give Facebook Groups a Try _____ 45

   Taking Advantage of Facebook Live ___ 54

Marketing on YouTube _____ 60

   Growing Your YouTube Channel _____ 60

   Improving the Performance of
   Your Videos _____ 68

   Generating Leads with YouTube _____ 71

Marketing on Instagram _____ 78

Taking Advantage of Instagram Stories _ 78

Driving the Best Results with Carousel
Posts _____ 88

IGTV for Businesses _____ 92

Your Influencer Marketing Strategy ____ 96

Marketing on Twitter_____ 105

Promoting in 280 Characters _____ 105

Twitter Advanced Search for Getting More
Leads _____ 108

Hosting a Twitter Chat _____ 111

The Ultimate Dos and Don'ts of Twitter
Marketing_____ 118

Marketing on LinkedIn _____ 122

Optimizing Your Page_____ 123

Promoting and Selling on LinkedIn_____ 125

Starting a LinkedIn Group_____ 127

LinkedIn as a Content Platform _____ 133

Tips for Getting More LinkedIn
Followers _____ 137

Marketing on Pinterest _____ 139

Quality Pins for More Saves_____ 139

Optimize and Engage for Success _____ 146

Leveraging Pinterest Marketing in
Steps _____ 150

Getting Started with Snapchat_____ 152

Setting Up the Account _____ 152

Adding Followers_____ 156

Taking Your Snaps _____ 157

Sharing Your Brand's Story _____ 158

Engage! _____ 161

Conclusion_____ 165

Introduction

Did you manage to create your social media accounts but got stuck on your way to successfully promoting your brand? If your business is already present on social media but you struggle to grow your following and get your audience to engage with your content, you are at the right place.

You don't have to try too hard and overly promote yourself in order to draw customers. You just need to funnel your posts and take the right action that has helped many small businesses grow huge. This book is packed with tried-and-true methods of attracting potential customers with scroll-stopping content that will bring value to your fan base. So, if you are wondering why your Instagram posts don't have as many likes as your competitor's account or why your YouTube videos go unnoticed, the answers can be found in this guide.

Providing you with advanced marketing tips and techniques that will bring you the social media fame that your brand deserves, this book will show you that having thousands of followers doesn't necessarily mean having thousands of dollars to spend.

Ready for your visually stunning journey that will lead you to tons of new customers and a well-established brand? Join me on this knowledgeable social media ride and learn how to take advantage of the social media platforms to help your business grow.

Social Media Marketing – The New Era of Brand Promoting

What is the first thing that comes to your mind when someone mentions *marketing*? Newspaper ads? Radio pitches? Boring TV commercials? Direct mail? Or even manipulation? In the past, this was the only way in which businesses could reach customers. In the golden years of television, all you had to do in order to promote your brand to the world was to have a giant budget. Huge budget plus your product on TV equaled a guaranteed hit. But high budgets were for the really successful companies. And even though the invention of cable did bring some extra marketing opportunities, for small businesses, promoting their brand to customers was nothing but a pipe dream. Fortunately, the birth of the Internet shook things up and created new and much more affordable ways for marketing and communicating in general.

It is true that traditional forms of marketing still exist, but unlike before, having a Newspaper ad today is not a main marketing strategy, but an additional promoting technique to help businesses further expand their audience reach. Things have changed significantly, even up to a point where having a huge budget doesn't necessarily mean instant success. Nor does having a celebrity promoting your brand. The key to successful marketing is satisfying thek customer's needs.

Now, the modern consumer has increased needs and higher expectations than people did back in the TV's golden era. When purchasing a product or a service, people expect to get a personalized buyer's experience. And, instead of just watching a TV commercial and heading to the store, people now have much more exciting ways to explore their options and embark on their buying journey.

Today, a shopper may decide to visit your online store, do a price research on their smartphone, check the product's reviews online, watch a testimonial video, or even solicit feedback from friends on social media, all in order to determine whether purchasing your product will be worth it. So, it's easy to understand why funneling your budget only to customer acquisition no longer satisfies these complex buyer journeys. In order to build an engagement with their customers that will lead to positive customer experience and brand advocacy, businesses are now faced with reaching the customers across many different channels. Most of these channels are found on *Social Media*.

The moment that social media became a hit, businesses jumped on the bandwagon on promoting their services there. Why? Because social media is where most of your customers are. Marketing on social media is the quickest and most cost-effective way to reach your target audience.

But unlike traditional marketing that allowed very limited marketing opportunities for companies smaller than the large corporations, social media marketing is, in fact, more beneficial for small businesses. Marketing on social media is not a strategy about gaining millions of followers but about having customers that are engaged.

The new era of marketing has surely changed in favor of small businesses. Here is how they have more advantages on social media than the large companies with 6-figure budgets:

Individual-eFocused. One of the biggest differences between large- and small-scale companies, is that small businesses are actively involved in their communities and heavily focused on individuals. Customers have much more appreciation for smaller businesses as they tend to foster solid communication with individual customers. Take advantage of that!

Joint Marketing Efforts. When small businesses join forces, it can result in a very profitable outcome. And the social media platforms offer a great way for businesses to collaborate on their marketing strategies. Offering discounts, coupons, and demos are all great examples of this kind of strategies. For instance, you may partner up with another business and each of you to offer a discount of 30% for the other brand's products when a purchase of a particular product of yours is made. That way the customer pays less, both businesses profit, and everybody's happy. Obviously, this should be done with neighboring business only, not competitors.

Benefits from Big Advertising. You don't have to do the advertising yourself in order to profit. Some large corporations actually hold events that you can leverage in your own promoting techniques. For instance, American Express holds a Small Business Saturday, which is an event that encourages customers to shop small. By only posting that you will participate in such an event, you get to reap the benefits with almost no hassle involved.

Personalized Experience. Did you know that more than half of the consumers say that they are more likely to shop from smaller businesses because of the personalized attention they get? Since large corporations don't get the time to provide a personalized experience to each customer, this is something that small businesses can leverage in their social media marketing strategies. When customers come to your business, take the time to really connect. Genuine and timely responses and taking the time to understand what the customer is looking for in order to provide the best service for them, are both great examples of personalized attention.

As you can see, social media really did change the one-dimensional and boring traditional way of marketing for the better. However, keep in mind that all of those well-known, tried-and-true strategies still very much apply to marketing, even on social media. Social media marketing may be the new marketing era, but it is still the same world.

Your Best Strategy for Marketing on Social Media

Embarking the social media marketing train unprepared can be a deadly journey. Many businesses open their social accounts on an ad hoc basis; just because they think it is expected of them to be present there. However, not being present is sometimes better than being active without fully understanding what to do and how to be engaged. In order to be able to reap the benefits that social media marketing provides (web traffic, reaching customers, spreading brand awareness, building up loyalty, etc.), you need a well-planned marketing strategy that will help you stand out and slay the competition.

And while it is true that every social media platform requires a unique approach and differently-optimized technique, there are a set number of steps that businesses should take on each platform, in order to create their best marketing strategy:

Step #1: Set SMART Goals

Being on social media without knowing why exactly you have signed up in the first place is not how you should start your social media marketing.

Having a set of goals that you wish to achieve is the best starting point for any marketing strategy. However, if your goals are set just for the sake of it, they may not help build up the most suitable strategy for you. To ensure that they are created with the purpose of finding the best marketing technique, your goals should fit into your plan as a whole, and most importantly, they should be set in a way in which you'd like your business to progress. For that purpose, -your goals should be SMART:

Specific – Specific and focused on identifying a concrete   outcome
Measurable – Defined success to evaluate progress and   strive   towards   its   achievement
Attainable – Challenging and yet reasonable to achieve
Relevant - Real and set to determine whether your efforts   are   worthwhile   to   you
Time-Bound - Realistic time frame for achieving your goal

Step #2: Understand Your Audience

Making assumptions can be dangerous. In order for you to provide value to your customers, you first need to know what it is that they are looking for. Keep in mind that every social media audience is different; you fan base on Instagram and your connections on LinkedIn want different things. Researching your audience prior to taking the plunge of promoting your brand is essential.

Luckily for you, there are many different tools that can help you take a glance at the newest social media demographic data to find the best approach for your social media platforms.

Step #3: Determine Your Metrics

Many businesses spend their time, money and effort promoting their brand, without stopping to take a look at how far they have gone. Regardless of the product or service you are trying to sell, the marketing strategy you take on social media should always be driven by data. The "likes" and number of followers you get are surely great to have, but if they do not turn out to be meaningful and result in customer engagement, they are really useless. Here are the metrics that matter the most when trying to understand whether your social media marketing strategy is successful:

Reach – The number of users that saw what you had shared. Check to see how far your reach actually spreads across the platform and whether it reaches the feeds of the audience.

Engagement – The number of interactions divided by the total number of impressions. This shows you what the audience thinks of you and whether they are willing to engage with your content.

Clicks – This represents the number of times people clicked on your content, logo, or the name of your company. When having a campaign running, these clicks are a great indicator of the things that encourage your audience to buy.

Organic and Paid Likes – These are the likes you get from paid or organic content, and they can be a great way to determine the type of content that attracts more audience and why.

Hashtag Performance – Everything related to hashtags can be found here. From the hashtags that are most associated with your business to the hashtag that brought the most engaged audience.

Sentiment – This measures the way in which your audience react to your content, hashtag, or overall brand. The sentiment digs a bit deeper and lets you know what people actually think about your brand and social media presence.

Step #4: Check Out the Competition

No matter what type of business you are trying to promote, chances are, the social media platforms are already packed with competition. Inspecting what your competition is offering to your target audience is a great way for you to determine what the weaknesses and strengths of the competitor brands are, in order to try and exploit them. Sneaky, right?

Go through their social media accounts and see what they are offering. What is their approach? What are they mostly focused on? What are the keywords that they rely on? Answering these questions will help you learn what is missing and how you can improve your strategy to offer your potential customers even better experience.

Step #5: Create Engaging Content

Social media is centered around content, so it's only understandable why posting suitable and engaging content of high-quality should be the heart of your social marketing strategy. But if you think that you can promote your brand in every single post and provide nothing but sales pitches to your followers in order to turn them into customers, you cannot be more wrong. 43% of social media users say that they will most likely unfollow businesses that try to hard to make a sell and are overly promotional of their brands. Instead, users want unique and genuine content that provides value.

Creating user-generated content for that purpose can be quite beneficial. By sharing popular hashtags, you will let your audience see a rawer side of you, without having to do any work, really.

When creating content, do not forget the magic of the visual. Our brain is wired to process images way faster than textual content, so even when you have a textual announcement to make, try to stick a cute photo alongside. Visual content gets shared 40% more than other content types, so create your content with that thought in mind.

Step #6: Post at the Right Times

In order for you to get the maximum engagement possible, you need to post your content at the times when your target audience is active the most. Of course, this depends on what your business is about and who your target audience actually is. For instance, if you are in the healthcare industry, the best time to post on Twitter is on Wednesday between 11 and 1 a.m. But, if you are in the Consumer Goods industry, then you should post on Saturday at 1 p.m. There are many factors involved when deciding on the right posting times on the social media platforms – from your industry sector to the age group and location of your target audience - and the truth is, calculating on your own can be quite overwhelming. Instead of doing everything manually and by yourself, invest in a good tech tool that will not only do all the work for you, but will also show flawless and highly-accurate results.

Step #7: Engage

Social media is the place to connect with people and interact. If you want to stand out and be successful, you shouldn't just broadcast your content to your audience, but engage with them on a regular basis, as well. Create a custom hashtag to encourage discussions and get more engagement from your audience, but be prepared to respond to every social mention of your brand to show users that your customers are your number one priority.

Ideally, you should respond to all customers' requests and inquiries within 4 hours, as that is the wait time that most users expect. The average response time is 10 hours, so make sure to be one of the businesses who doesn't live their customers waiting for a response.

Step #8: Track and Improve

No matter how much you plan your strategies, things rarely go as expected. You will need to track your most relevant metrics in order to know just how your marketing strategy is progressing. That is the only way in which you can learn what works and what should be improved in order to adapt your technique and bring more value to your customers for a successful promotion.

Prioritizing the Top Platform for Your Brand

One of the main reasons why people fail to establish a successful social media marketing is the fact that they prioritize the wrong social media platform. It doesn't matter if most of your friends are active on Facebook. That is not an indicator that you should bet your entire budget on Facebook advertising. Just because most of the people you know are addicted to a particular social media network doesn't mean that majority of your target audience have active accounts there.

Even though it is required that you have a strong presence on each of the most popular social media platforms, you need to pinpoint exactly which one of them you need to focus on the most. Otherwise, you might be spending your resources on an account that garners insufficient customer engagement. To provide value to your customers, you need to allocate your resources more efficiently. Having a hard time deciding which social media platform works best for your business? Read on to determine where you should be spending your budget the most.

Facebook

Facebook is the biggest social media platform and should be approached as such. Whether your audience is most active there or not, a Facebook presence is a definite must. But is the majority of your target audience really there?

Facebook is best for B2C businesses, and in some cases B2B as well. The top industries that thrive from Facebook marketing are:

- Fashion

- E-commerce

- Real Estate

- Health and Wellness

- Retail

- Sports

- Marketing

- Auto

- Entertainment

- News and Information

In 2018, the most common age demographic was from 25 to 34. The target age and gender are both men and women aged from 25 to 55+.

Did you know that Facebook is considered to be an SEO signal on a local level? That means that search engines check your Facebook profile in order to give relevant local search results.

Twitter

Twitter is also best for B2C businesses, although some B2Bs may also be at an advantage at this platform. The top industries that benefit from Twitter are:

- News and Information

- Travel and Hospitality

- Retail

- Health and Wellness

- Telecom

- Sports

- Finance

- E-commerce

- Sports

The most active audience on Twitter are both men and women from 18 to 29 years of age.

Twitter is the perfect spot for customer service. Whenever a customer comes across an issue with a product or service they cannot solve, they Tweet the business hoping to get the solution. Twitter has definitely become the central hub for customers, so make sure to take advantage of his platform and show off your expertise to the world.

Did you know that 93 percent of the people on Twitter who follow SMBs plan to actually buy products or services from the small and medium-sized businesses that they follow?

Instagram

Instagram is also best for B2C businesses and if you have got a visual product, then this is probably the best platform for marketing your brand. On the first glance, Instagram may seem like nothing more than an app for sharing photos, but this platform seriously packs a punch, especially with the younger audience, as 64 percent of the active Instagram profiles are aged from 18 to 29 years. Women are slightly more active on this platform than men, but keep in mind that that's shifting.

The industries that benefit the most from marketing on Instagram are:

- Fashion

- Travel and Hospitality

- Arts and Crafts

- Beauty

- Food and Beverage

- Photography

- Event Planning

- Health and Wellness

- E-commerce

- Auto

Did you know that 80% of all Instagram accounts follow a business? And what's even more interesting is the fact that 72% of them actually say that they have made a purchase of a product that they saw on Instagram.

Pinterest

Again, best for B2C businesses, Pinterest is a platform that every hobbyist is addicted to. Whether they are planning an event, remodeling their house, or saving yummy recipes, Pinterest is the paradise for everyone who is looking for inspiration and new ideas.

The most active group there are women between 18 and 45 years.

Pinterest is the perfect platform for these industries:

- Health and Wellness

- Retail

- Home and Garden

- Beauty

- Event Planning

- Fashion

- Food and Beverage

- Travel and Hospitality

- Arts and Crafts

- E-commerce

Did you know that whopping 87 percent of all active pinners have actually made purchases because of this platform?

LinkedIn

LinkedIn is a platform that is best for both B2B and B2C employment. If you are a business-to-business, then LinkedIn should definitely be the social media platform that you should prioritize.

The most active target group here are both men and women from 25 to 45 years of age.

The top industries that thrive the most on LinkedIn are:

- Financial

- Manufacturing

- Employment

- Legal

- Education

- Marketing

- Health and Wellness

- Science and Technology

- IT

- Professional Services

Did you know that the audience on LinkedIn actually has twice the purchasing power than the average audience on the web?

Another platform that you simply cannot afford not to be present on is **YouTube**. Although YouTube is surely different than the previously mentioned ones, it has proven to be of tremendous benefit for businesses of any kind. And while YouTube shouldn't be your main marketing platform, a strong presence there can be of extraordinary value for your business.

Marketing on Facebook

Facebook is, without a doubt, the most popular social media platform today. It is the place where people of all ages or backgrounds gather, in order to share details of their lives with close friends and family, as well as to stay in touch with people that they don't get to see often.

But the fact that this is what Facebook is mainly used for shouldn't discourage you. Quite the contrary. Having more than 2.3 billion of active monthly users gathered at one place is just what businesses need in order to raise awareness and grow a large customer community. Whether you are planning to use this platform for your main marketing strategy or not, it doesn't matter. Facebook is where most social media users are, and your place should definitely be among them.

Think Like a Follower

You cannot possibly expect for your marketing strategy to work if you fail to understand the reason why people may decide to follow you. Before you get all crazy with your posts and somehow expect an impossible level of engagement, it is important for you to know exactly what your fans are expecting from you.

Sure, the people who follow your brand on Facebook are definitely more likely to purchase a product or service from you. But keep in mind that they do not hit the 'like' button to buy from you. They are following your brand on Facebook because:

They Want a Discount – Most of your followers are expecting to receive some discounts at some points. Of course, this doesn't mean that you should give out coupons every day, but it will be beneficial if you make discounts a part of your marketing strategy.

They Want Updates and News – Fans follow brands also in order to stay updated with the latest products and services.

They Are Following Someone's Recommendation – A considerable amount of your followers will most likely hit 'follow' because a friend has recommended your brand and they are looking for the same positive experience.

They Are Looking for Like-Minded People – Many people follow businesses, news stations or shows, because they are looking for a way to talk about the things they are interested in with other enthusiasts.

They Want to Be Entertained – People want to be amused and entertained. You cannot possibly expect that your business-related stats will encourage your fans to engage. You need to provide them with engaging visual content in order for them to be interested in what you have to offer.

They Want to Express Loyalty – Most of the customers that enjoy your product/service online will most likely want to seek you online and become your follower. Believe it or not, many of your followers will be people just wanting to show support for the brand they believe in.

They Want to Ask a Question –With the rise of social media, who wants to dial customer service and spend their time waiting on hold? Most of the customers that want to ask your business a question will become your follower and do it online.

They Want to Give a Feedback - Many people will choose to become your follower in order to leave their honest feedback regarding your services or products.

Knowing what your followers are looking for and why they have decided to follow your brand the first place, is a great advantage that will be pretty helpful in strengthening the relationship with your customers.

Boosting Your Facebook Page

Assuming that you already have an up-and-running Facebook page, the next step is to give it a few boosts and start using it actively in order to reach to the people that matter the most to your brand.

Improving the Visibility

Optimizing your Facebook page in order to improve its visibility is (alongside creating quality content, obviously) the most important thing when it comes to marketing your brand on Facebook. Your business is competing with millions of other brands on this platform and, in order for you to stand out, you need to make sure that, when searching for something similar (whether on Facebook or in the Search Engines), people will come across your brand. Here are 4 incredibly important optimization tips that you cannot afford to miss out on:

#1: Combine the Name of Your Page with a Keyword

Choosing the right name for your page is of crucial importance for the visibility of your brand on Facebook. But, don't confuse this with your username. Your username is the identifier for your page on Facebook, and it is a unique name found at the end of your URL. It is showed in your page under the '@'symbol. This is not your page name. Your page name is the title of your Facebook Page that is shown in the search results.

If your business is unique and doesn't share common words with similar businesses or is already a well-established brand (think Quaker Oats or Ben & Jerry's), you can use nothing but your business name as a name for your Page. But, if your business is niched or has recently been founded, then you need to take a different approach. If that is the case, you might want to consider combining your business name with a keyword or a keyword phrase. Why? Because people who are looking to make a purchase online use keywords, not brand names.

For instance, if you own a pastry shop called Violet Delights you may find that there is already a 'Violet Delights' page on Facebook under the Fashion Designer and Boutique Store category. That means that using only your business name is probably not a good idea. Instead, combine it with some keywords to optimize your visibility. Naming your Page something like: Violet Delights London Pastry Shop, will make sure that your page shows up in related searches for pastry shops in your area.

#2: Customize Search Snippets

Your 'About' section is the place where you should let people know what your business is all about, where they can find you, how to get in touch with you, and things of that sort. But, what you probably didn't know is that the text you provide in this section can also be used for forming search snippets that will show up in the results on both Facebook and Google.

Try to share the information about your business in a way that can be easily converted to a search snippet. Try to add the most important info in a short and up-to-the-point format that people can see in their search results even before clicking on your Page in order to draw more attention to your Facebook Page.

#3: Complete the Info to Make Your Business Visible Locally

Remember how we said that Facebook is a local SEO signal? That means that when you go online to search for pastries shops, Google and Facebook consider your location first and display the pastries shops that can be found in your area.

This feature is especially beneficial for small, local businesses. In order to make sure that your Facebook Page will be shown on the local search results, you need to first complete all of the relevant info for your business such as: Country, City, Address, Zip Code, Phone Number, Working Hours, etc.

#4: Incorporate Keywords in the Content You Post

Keywords, keywords, keywords. Once you begin your social media marketing journey, keywords will be the term that you will constantly bump across. I, personally, cannot stress the importance of using relevant keywords enough. Why? Because it is impossible for you to gain organic or paid reach if you do not know what your potential customers are searching for in order to find the services that you provide. Once you know the keywords that are relevant for your business (you can use tools such as Google AdWords Keyword Planner), you should start incorporating them in your posts, the image and video descriptions, titles, etc.

However, using relevant keywords may also turn out to be not that productive if the competitions for those specific keywords is high. In that case, you will have to find other relevant phrases that are not used as often. https://moz.com/explorer is a great tool that can get the job done for you.

Enhancing the Timeline Tactically

Even though your Facebook page may be pretty much set up, without some tweaking it may look pretty bland. There are some finishing touches that you need to add in order for your page to be more appealing to your audience. Here are three simple things you can do to your timeline in order to enhance the look of your Facebook Page and create a stronger relationship with your audience:

Pin Content

Pinning Content is just what the name suggests. Pinning your most important posts and making them stick to the top of your timeline, which means that, even though you may continue posting, that post will still be top post your audience will see when they look at your Page. Your posts will stay *sticky*, until you decide to unpin them.

This is great for highlighting special product announcements, great discounts, promotional campaigns, or other limited offers. But what's even greater about this feature is that it gives you a perfect opportunity to welcome new followers and tell what your business is all about in a fun and engaging way. If you can, make a "welcome video" and pin it to the top with a short message like "Welcome to our page! If you are new here, take a minute to watch our short but helpful video". Or,

34

create a great welcome sign and pin the image to the top. The welcome message can be especially beneficial if you are just starting your Facebook journey.

Keep in mind that you can only pin one post at a time. Each pinned post will stay at the top for up to a week (of course, unless you decide to unpin it before that). To pin a post, just click on the pencil icon in the top right corner of your post. From the drop-down menu, select **'Pin to Top'**. To unpin the post, click on the pencil icon and select the unpin option.

Highlight a Post

Highlighting a post means expanding a certain status update across your Timeline, by taking up the space of both of the columns. Posts are highlighted with the purpose of drawing attention to some of your most important posts.

The fact that you can have many highlighted posts on your timeline makes a great highlighting strategy that can help you draw more traffic. Highlighted posts are great for grabbing the follower's attention when you are trying to introduce a new program or a service. You can create a series of images and have them roll out over a set period of time.

Another great strategy would be to highlight every customer testimonial. Whenever you see a customer share positive feedback about your product or services, turn that into a post, add an image of that customer, and highlight that post to make it really stand out.

To highlight a post, click on the star icon found in the top right corner of a post. To undo the highlighting, just unclick the star icon and the post will be no longer highlighted.

Keep in mind: Pinned posts will most likely make your posts more visible as they appear at the top of your timeline. Highlighted posts do not stay at the top, but are highlighted chronologically, and are pushed down across the Timeline with each new post that appears. The advantage of the highlighted posts, however, is that they have no time limitations. Also, have in mind that you cannot choose both pinning and highlighting for the same post. For each post, you are allowed only one option.

Create Milestones

Milestones are the perfect way for you to share the story of your business to your audience, through the power of images and words. The milestones are uploaded in chronological order and can appear anywhere on the Timeline, depending on the time and take you set. For instance, you can create a milestone for the day that your business was founded, even if that happened a hundred years ago. Obviously, this will be the oldest milestone.

To create a milestone, select '**Event, Milestones +**' from the drop-down menu in the status update bar. By default, each milestone will be highlighted and then stretched across your Timeline.

Milestones are a great way for businesses to tell a story, but most brands fail to understand that the milestones can also be a part of their marketing strategy. Keep in mind that the more meaning you assign to the milestones, the more traction you will be able to see:

Include an Image – Do not just say that your business was founded in 1965. Include an engaging image that will capture the attention of your followers. If you need to, scan some old newspapers or photos to give your audience a more transparent look into the history of your business.

Include a Call-to-Action – Make sure to encourage your customers to find out more. Include a call-to-action by pasting a link that leads to more info about the created milestone. By doing so, you encourage people to take an action and potentially purchase a product or service.

By turning pins, highlights, and milestones into a strategy, you are more likely to use these amazing features on a regular basis, which can not only visually transform your Facebook Page and bring you more followers, but it will also encourage the audience you have to become more engaged with your content.

Take Advantage of Apps

To make your Page even more appealing to the eye, take advantage of different apps that allow you to share slides, poll your community, and approach your marketing strategy form an even more interactive   angle. However, make sure not to get too crazy with all the bells and whistles. Those apps may turn out to put your followers off if they are used poorly. Be moderate with these extras and try not to go overboard.

Your Strategy for Encouraging Engagement

Facebook pages have become even more powerful than TV. Large businesses (think Coca Cola) can reach more people with a simple post update than with a TV commercial. And the best part? Facebook posts are free (unless you are paying for the advertisement, of course, in which case it is still a lot cheaper).

The content you post on Facebook should:

- Create brand awareness
- Establish expertise
- Drive traffic
- Have multiple goals
- Increase your community
- Drive sales without being a sales pitch
- Be proofread and well-constructed
- Be visually engaging
- Be on topic
- Be light and upbeat

However, once you start sharing your content with your audience, you will see that posting is easy. The part that is tricky, is having your followers engage with your content. In order for your audience to respond, they need to be compelled to do so. Attracting engagement may seem like a hard task, but with a few techniques under your belt, you can easily form a strong interactive relationship with your audience.

Structure Well to Get Answers

Sometimes, the best strategy lies in the way you create your content. Your posts should carry open questions that will attract your audience to comment and share their opinion. Your questions should be:

- Open – They should carry a discussion that is open-ended

- Easy – They shouldn't require too much thinking in order to attract a larger group. The answers should be given rather impulsively

- Timely – To get higher engagement, tend to ask questions that follow a hot topic or trend

Your questions should never be:

- Political – You shouldn't take a side as a brand, but if you are discussing a political issue without taking one, you will most likely be accused of not taking one. The secret formula is to steer clear from discussing politics

- Complicated – Philosophical questions are not for your brand's business page. The questions that require research are usually not answered on Facebook.

- Loaded – If your questions are pretty much self-explanatory and don't really require an answer, no one will bother to comment on them

Make Them Ask Questions

The tried-and-true way to make your audience interested in engaging with your brand is to give them the power to feel in charge. And the best way to do so is to provide your followers with the opportunity to ask you questions.

This will work the best if you create a topic or a theme for the questions, set an end date, and explain when and who will answer the questions. Just sure to put the right person for the job under the spotlight here in order to give the right answers.

You can present the answers in a video, a document, or even stream a Facebook Live streaming where the questions will be answered live, to further increase the engagement.

Use the Emojis

The best way in which you can illustrate sentiment is by using emojis in your posts. The use of emojis will not only make your content more attractive, but it will also give your audience the impression that your business is friendly. Those posts that include emojis have higher chances for like, comment, and share.

Ask for Feedback

You may think that asking your audience for feedback may seem as begging, but the truth is, people like to be included. By asking your followers to share their feedback on a certain product or service, you let them know that you value their opinion, and that is something that can do wonders for the level of engagement on your Page.

Generate Messenger Connections with a Discount in Your Post

The bots in Facebook Messenger are increasingly gaining in popularity. There are many tools for small businesses that provide you with the opportunity to automatically respond to a comment with a bot (https://manychat.com/ is a great tool for this purpose). But besides being used to enhance the shopping experience or give updates, you can take advantage of this AI communication by giving away discount. What am I talking about? For instance, a great tactic for increasing the engagement is asking people to comment on a post and giving them a coupon or discount in return. That way, many people will take the bait and engage with your content. Once the comment is shared, messenger bots will automatically reward them with the voucher.

Who doesn't like free stuff? Offers like this will encourage most of your followers to comment, but what's even more important for your marketing, is the fact that the traffic will send a signal to Facebook's algorithm that quality content is shared, which will only increase the visibility of your post.

Give Your Fans a Shout-Out

Spotted a follower wearing your company's t-shirt or drinking your coffee? Share the picture posted by your followers to show your audience how much you appreciate their positive feedback. But, before you hit the 'share' button, make sure to ask for permission from the original poster, and obviously, thank the contributor.

By thanking your audience for your loyalty, you will create a goodwill feeling that will most likely result not only in the engagement on that particular post but on your other content as well.

Create Facebook Events

Facebook events are the best way to show your audience that you are constantly working on something to provide them with more value. Creating Facebook events will not only let your followers know that you want to keep your community tight but also will allow you to gauge the interest of your audience.

Facebook events can include:

- Sale

- Tweet-Up (a meet-up on Twitter) or a Twitter Chat

- Party

- Conference

- Contest

- Webinar

The best thing about events is the fact that they are easy to set u, and you get to invite everyone that follows your brand on Facebook:

1. Click on **'Events'** found in the left menu of your home page.

2. Select + **Create Event.**

3. At this point, you can either choose to **Create a Public Event** if you want your event to be seen by everyone, even those that are not your followers, or **Create a Private Event**, if you want only the people you invite to be able to see the event. Note that whatever option you choose, you will not be able to change it later.

4. Fill in the details such as the name of the event, the time and date, as well as write a compelling description.

5. Click on **'Create'**. You will then be redirected to a page where you should invite the people you want to invite to the even.

One of the biggest Facebook marketing mistakes that small businesses make is using Facebook Events to spam. If you invite people to events every other day, you will not only lose your brand's credibility and your existing audience, but you are also at risk of having your Facebook account suspended or shut down.

Give Facebook Groups a Try

Besides having a Facebook Page – which is absolutely necessary in order to market your brand on Facebook – as a business, you should also think about trying Facebook Groups as well. Facebook groups are different than Pages in a way that they allow only 5,000 people (Pages can have millions of followers), and that the conversation in Facebook Groups is a bit more expansive. Facebook Groups have dozens of conversations going a on daily basis and are the perfect opportunity for you to position your brand and find new customers.

With Facebook Groups you have two options:

1. You can join an existing Facebook Group with your personal profile

2. You can create your own Facebook Group

Joining a Facebook Group

If you think about skipping this option as you don't see how your business can benefit from this, you cannot be more wrong. Joining an existing Facebook Group that is managed by someone else, gives you the perfect chance for you to create awareness for your brand by being helpful. People tend to ask a lot of questions in groups. Find the ones where you can share your skills and expertise in order to resolve someone's issue, become a member and spread brand awareness. You can do this by giving outright answers, sharing a video, links to blog posts, or even mentioning your own services. This will not only let people know about your brand, but it will also reward you with extra followers.

Here is how you can become a member of groups and engage with people who you believe might be potential customers:

1. Log into your personal Facebook Profile.

2. Click on the **'Groups'** tab found in the left 'Explore' section of your Home page.

3. Once you are automatically sent to the **'Discover Groups'** page, you will see suggested groups by Facebook, based on the groups you've already liked or those that your friends participate in.

4. Once you find a group you wish to join, click the **'Join Button'**.

Keep in mind that Groups and Pages are different. Unlike simply clicking the 'Like' button and becoming a fan of a Page, you will have to be accepted in order to become a member of a group (unless it is Public). Also, some groups will ask you to give your answer to a few questions before you send your request. Once your request has been approved, a notification will be sent to you. You can then start a conversation or join existing ones.

Creating Your Own Facebook Group

As much as it is beneficial to be a member of a group that is managed by someone else, keep in mind that you have to play by others' rules. Deciding to create your own Facebook Group means you get to control the entire group, as well as gives you the opportunity to see the group as you see fit and for the purpose that helps your brand the most.

But, before you begin building your group, you will first need to decide what kind of the group you wish to create. There are three different ways in which most businesses use groups:

To Create a Community Around Products

Most of the business groups are created with the purpose of giving the customers a bonus for purchasing a particular product or service. By creating such a group where your paid customers will be members of, you reward them by making them feel privileged and exclusive. You can use these groups to give them additional tips or training for the products or services purchased.

To Establish Authority

You can also have a special group created especially for your email subscribers where you can share articles, tips, and tutorials on how to use your product or services.

To Build a Community Around a Specific Topic

You don't have to use your company's name for the name of your group. Instead, your group can be created to reflect a certain topic that your business has expertise in. For instance, if you are selling spices, one idea for your business is to create a group called "Spicy Homemade Recipes" and use your spices as ingredients for creating the delicacies. That way your customers will be given plenty of inspiration on how to use your products, and other people who are fans of spicy cuisine can also be drawn to your Group and Page and will most likely become potential customers.

Now that you know why you will use your Group, let's see how you can successfully create one.

Creating the Group

Log into your personal Facebook profile, and click on the **'Group'** button found in the left sidebar. Next, select the green **'Create Group'** option. A '**Create New Group**' dialogue box will appear, and you will be prompted to name your group, add some people, and select the privacy settings. *Important: You have to have at least one person to add to the group in order to create it!*

Depending on the goal of your business, your group can be:

Public – In Public Facebook Groups, the content is visible to anyone who decides to check the group out. Anyone can join a public Group and anyone can see the posts there. If your goal is to build a community around a specific topic, then a Public Group is perhaps the best choice.

Closed – Unlike with Public Groups, if someone wants to join a Closed Facebook Group, their request must be accepted by the Group administrator first. Here, the content can be seen only by the members of the Closed Group. Closed Group is the most popular type of Facebook Groups for businesses, as it creates a perfect opportunity for you to be picky about the people you let in, and ensures that no one other than the selected audience can get educated with your tips and tutorials for free.

Secret – In Secret Facebook Groups, it is not only the content that is secret, but the Group itself. Only the members can see the posts and the Group isn't listed in search results. The Secret Facebook Groups are best for businesses who are looking for a way to establish the authority of their business. These groups are created only for specific members and are a great way for your business to provide coaching. If you want to, you can even have your members pay a monthly fee to be a part of your Group.

Now that you have chosen the privacy level of your Group, click on **'Create'**. Your Group is now ready. All you need to do now is to load images and take care of the setting preferences and images.

Customizing the Group

Once your Group is all set up, the first thing you need to do is add a cover image. The recommended size is 828 x 315 pixels. Once the image appears, click on it, and add a description and the rules for the group.

Then, click on **'...'** in order to select the type of your Group. This obviously depends on your purpose. Would you like to educate, provide your audience with customer support, or create your group around a specific business' event? You can pick from Buy and Sell, Events and Plans, Family, Custom, Travel, Project, Support, Neighbors, etc.

Once you choose the type, the next step is to add your location, tags, web address and other contact info.

Now that your Group is ready to go, start posting. It is recommended to write down a post with the rules of your Group and pin it to the top.

Invite People to Join

The first mistake that most small businesses make, is the fact that they usually invite their friends and family to join first. As beneficial as they are to increase the number of followers on your Facebook Page, for your Group, your personal contacts may not be the best fit. Why? Because they usually are not paying customers. Your goal here should be to focus on the people that your Group will serve. Here are some tips that can help you find encourage the right people to join:

-   Send an email to your subscribers introducing your Group and encouraging them to join

- Share the Group on your other social media platforms

- Invite the visitors of your website to join your Facebook Group

- Add a button on your website that will lead your visitors to your Group

- On your lead magnet's thank-you page, add an invitation for your visitors to join

Curate Content

Before you can find content to share on your Group, you will first have to determine what type should the content be. What will your strategy be? To sell? To create a support group? To entertain? Once you make sure you are clear on that, you can find relevant content that is trending to share with your members.

Google News – If you want to share the most recent news article, there isn't the best place to look at, really.

https://buzzsumo.com/ - This gem will show you what the hottest topics are at the moment. Also, you can refine your search by searching for specific topics that are relevant for your group.

The most important thing is to stay as updated as possible and share topics that your Group members will be interested in interacting with.

Encourage Engagement

No strategy will be successful unless it yields in audience engagement. To make sure that your content will spark interaction, take advantage of some of these tips:

Tutorials – Make sure to post at least one tutorial video per week to keep your members updated with the latest product/service developments.

Polls – Struggling to find a new idea? Ask your members. Polls are a great way to check the audience's opinion as well as to get inspired.

Challenges – Challenges are perhaps the most attractive interactions among group members. Design a challenge of some sort and ask your members to join. You can even invite your members to work with you on a challenge, which is especially beneficial if your business provides services.

Live Q&As – A once-a-week live session for asking and answering questions is a great way to keep your Group members involved.

Daily Theme Prompts – Prompts allow people to post about a specific theme every day. Ask your members to post photos of your product/service. This will not only give them an opportunity to share something about themselves, but will also further expand the awareness for your brand.

Tip: As your Group grows, you may not be able to monitor and post actively. For that purpose, you should consider hiring a community manager to take care of that. Most groups' managers are the most active members of the groups. Look inside and find the ideal candidate.

Taking Advantage of Facebook Live

Think Facebook Live is just another social media vanity project? Well, think again because Facebook Live is just the thing your business needs in order to interact with customers in a more humane way. Unlike your regular video posts where you can just sit and hope that someone will comment, Facebook Live is not a one-way thing. Here, your audience is engaged to interact. In fact, it is the engagement that they find so appealing that makes Facebook Live so popular.

Broadcasting Live

There are two ways in which you can broadcast Live on Facebook. Through your Facebook profile and with the help of the Mentions app.

To stream Live <u>from your profile</u>, tap the 'Publish' option from your Facebook Page, and click on the **'Live'** icon. Once that option is chosen, in your status update bar, write down the description for the broadcast. This is the title of the Facebook Live and it is what will go out in the notifications and in the feed.

You will also have the option to choose the audience that you will broadcast to. You can either make it public, select only a group of people, or choose to be viewed by everyone who follows you. Then, click on **'Go Live'**. This is when the streaming will begin.

During your streaming, you will see the number of people who are viewing live, as well as the live comments that people are sending. This makes a perfect option for Q&As because you get to answer their questions in real time, which is what most customers appreciate the most.

After your broadcast is over, it will be saved on your Timeline just like any other video post.

To broadcast Live <u>through the Mentions app</u>. The process is pretty straightforward. Just, open the app, click on **'Post'**, and then select the **'Live Video'** option. The only difference here is that, unlike with your Facebook Page, the app doesn't give you the option to select your audience, as everything becomes public on your Page.

<u>Improving Your Streaming</u>

As beneficial as it is, if not done properly, Facebook Live can only make your business look unprofessional if caught unaware or unprepared. Here are some tips for you to improve your broadcast and provide high-quality streaming to your audience:

Have a Focus – The last thing you need is to be rambling in front of your audience live. For that purpose, be prepared in advance and have an outline of the things that you wish to talk about. Staying focused on the reason why you are streaming in the first place will help your broadcast seem natural and attract followers to engage.

Have a Compelling Title – Keep in mind that when people get notified that your business is about to go live, they only get the title of your broadcast. So, create your title with that in mind. Make sure it is a real attention-grabber that will encourage people to watch.

Use Both Cameras – If you are streaming from your Smartphone, make sure to use both the front and back cameras. No one wants to see you the camera move all the time, by toggling back and forth between the cameras on your phone, you will provide a much better video, even if one camera is of lower capacity.

Have a Great Audio – You can choose to speak clearly and loudly and that would be fine. However, it is recommended that you use a high-quality microphone for this purpose in order to provide a video of an even higher quality. Whatever you decide, the most important thing is to avoid broadcasting from a place where there are a lot of busy background noises.

Include a CTA – Ending your broadcast with a call-to-action is the most tactical way to finish your stream, as that way you direct your audience to a specific place. Whether it is to visit your website or share their thoughts on another post, the point is for the engagement not to end with the stream but to keep the audience as interactive as possible.

Edit the Videos

Once the streaming is over and the video is posted on your Timeline, you can choose to edit it just as you would edit any other video post. To do so, click on the date near the post and then select the **'Edit'** option.

Choose the Right Thumbnail – Facebook will give you ten different image options to be the thumbnail for your video, but you can also choose to upload your own, custom-made one. Unless Facebook's images are excellent, the latter option is recommended.

Choose the Category – Click on the **'Video Category'** and choose the right category for your video from the drop-down menu.

Include a Call-to-Action – Shop Now, Sign Up, and Learn More, are just some of the options that Facebook gives you to include as CTAs to encourage your customers to further engage. Since you've probably included a CTA in the video itself, make sure that this call-to-action matches the one from the streaming.

Increase the Reach – To further amplify your reach and become more visible, you may want to think about creating a video ad from your broadcast, through the Ads Manager.

Reusing the Stream

Just like with your other content, your Facebook Live broadcast should be used in as many different places as possible. The best way to do so is to write a blog post covering the most important things discussed in the broadcast. After having a good piece of content written, think about embedding the Facebook Live post or just adding the video.

You can then share the blog post across your other social media platforms to boost the audience engagement there.

I personally recommend embedding the Facebook Live post because that will get you more views on the video which will show on your Facebook page, which may result in even more followers.

Marketing on YouTube

You may think that your sheer presence on social media and the fact that you are posting regular content on YouTube are enough for you to gain thousands of views and a crowd that is willing to comment and engage with your videos, but once you begin marketing your brand on YouTube, you will soon realize that marketing success on YouTube goes beyond posting explainer and testimonial videos.

In order for your channel to attract many followers that plan on engaging with your videos, you will have to approach marketing more strategically. This chapter will give you some advanced tips on how to enhance your YouTube marketing journey.

Growing Your YouTube Channel

Your YouTube content should be optimized at every stage in order for it to compel users to watch, and more importantly, further engage with your videos. Having the next tactics up your sleeve may be just what you need to give your channel a boost and grow your following:

Make the Video Production Process Sustainable

Although this one goes without saying, the production's workflow is often the least tackled process in the making of videos. You may have a Hollywood-like budget to spend on your videos, but if it takes you too long to produce, your expensive videos are not going to grow your channel.

Regardless of the type of business you are trying to promote and the kind of video you want to film, you should know exactly what you want to achieve with your content and strive to develop and post it on a regular basis.

If you are serious about your YouTube marketing, then you might want to invest in a tiny video studio. It doesn't have to be anything fancy. A quiet place with a nice background, a camera that is ready to roll, and a microphone of high quality are enough for you to be ready to shoot at all times.

Hook Them Up from the Start

People start watching a video from the beginning, and if the beginning fails to sweep them off their feet, they will likely just go back to their silly cat videos instead. Strive to begin your videos with a great hook. For instance, if you are filming a project, make sure to show the end result first. For instance, if your video is for a cake recipe, show the baked and decorated cake first, to give the audience a taste of what they should expect to get by watching the whole thing.

Keep Your Opening Credits Short

Don't make your audience lose interest because of your long opening credit. Keeping mind that your followers have short attention spans, so make sure to have theirs hooked. Also, because long opening credit sequences are boring, people will be discouraged from clicking on another video of yours just to avoid watching the long opening again.

Instead, keep your opening short. Make it upbeat, punchy, and most importantly, not longer than 5 seconds.

Cut the Distractions Out of Your Videos

No matter howl prepared you are, chances are, when filming your videos, your mind will block at some point. Long pauses or bouncing from subject to subject can cause your audience to shift their view to the other videos in the recommendation sidebar instead. In order to keep them interested in what you have to say, you need to be interesting.

Once your video is filmed, watch it carefully and really pay attention to the details. Is it engaging enough to keep your audience compelled? If you veer from the subject too much, refilm it. If not, enhance it with some video editors that will allow you to smoothly cut from one shot to another.

https://www.openshot.org is a great free tool that can help you edit your videos. The whole point is to make sure you are engaging and give your audience a reason to click away.

Improve Your Watch Time with Longer Videos

This may contradict the previous "keep your openings short" statement, given the fact that people have short attention spans, however, if your videos are to-the-point and engaging, longer duration can actually lead to more watch time, which will, in turn, enhance your content in the YouTube's algorithm.

Of course, the video should be longer if it makes sense to talk for minutes on that specific topic. The point still remains that you shouldn't come as boring or cause your followers to click away. The rule of a thumb is that videos between 7 and 15 minutes in length perform the best.

Use Older Successfully-Proven Tactics

Each of your videos will perform differently, and the truth is, you cannot possibly make them all to be successful. However, you can use the same tactics in order to strive to recreate the thing that makes your audience watch your top videos.

Dive into YouTube Analytics and see which videos perform the best. Then, spend some time watching and comparing, and try to find patterns among them. Is the subject similar? Are they edited with the same style? Is your mood brighter? Take notes of the similarities and try to incorporate them in future videos to boost up your ranking.

Your highest-converting videos can be found in the Creator Studio. Simply, go to **'Analytics'→ 'Subscribers'** and then select **'YouTube Watch Page'**.

Develop Series

There is nothing that can improve your watch time like having videos that people will want to binge watch. Series playlists are the best way for you to create a great binge-watching experience for your audience, but in order to create them, you need to have uploaded videos as a series.

Your series can be developed based on the type of videos that has performed well, however, it is best to have more than one series, each of them covering a specific topic. For instance, if you have testimonial and explainer videos, create two series for each of the two topics, but also, use a different style for the thumbnails as well. That way your viewers can easily know what the video is about just by taking a quick look at the thumbnail image.

Using videos as a series means that if a viewer clicks on the video, YouTube will automatically have your next video to be Up Next at the top of the list of recommendations. The next video will automatically play after the current one is over, unless the viewer has turned off their AutoPlay option.

In order for you to turn a playlist into a series playlist, open **'Video Manager'**. Go to **'Playlists'** and click on the edit button found on the right of the playlist that you wish to change. Finally, click on **'Playlist Settings'** → **'Set as Official Series for This Playlist'**.

Go with the 'Hub, Hero, Help' Strategy

Using three different types of videos in your content strategy can be of significant importance for your YouTube channel. By choosing the 'Hub, Hero, Help' strategy, your videos have three different goals:

1. To serve the community of the channel
2. To be shareable
3. To perform well in search

Hub Videos are focused on the community and are created with the purpose to strengthen the bond between you and your viewers, as well as with your viewers with each other. In these videos, you should respond to comments, post live, or even share personal stories.

Hero Videos are videos that are specifically designed to yield success. They are mostly focused on a hot subject, such as a news event or an upcoming holiday. Those videos are designed to encourage people to share them.

Help Videos to provide content that is easy-to-search and provides value that is actionable. Troubleshooting videos, DIY projects, and general how-to videos all fall under this category. If you want to find topics that people search the most at the moment, check out Google Trends and get the inspiration for your latest Help Video.

Adding these three types of videos to your content calendar can be quite beneficial, but only if you post them at different intervals. For instance, the best strategy is to upload one Hub Video each month, to post Hero Videos every 3 months, and to upload Help Videos on a weekly basis.

Team Up with Other YouTubers

You cannot do everything alone, and neither can the rest of the small businesses promoting their brands on YouTube. Collaborating with other YouTubers and filming videos together is the best tactic to expose yourself to people who'd never have heard of your brand.

When two content creators collaborate with each other, that creates an endorsement. The video alone may be a good enough reason for the other brand's viewers to check your channel out, and click the 'Subscribe' button. Some of the hugest YouTube creators cross-promote their content, so why shouldn't you?

First things first, you need to find the perfect collaborator. Ideally, the other YouTuber should have a slightly large channel than yours, but don't obsess with the channel's size too much. The important thing is for the collaborator to offer a different content to a similar audience. For instance, if you are selling spices, you might want to consider teaming up with a local farmer and create recipes promoting their fresh ingredients and your unique spices.

There are tools who can help you find the right collaborator. https://socialblade.com/ offers a great way for you to compare metrics and find the perfect match. When selecting the right candidate, look at their location, gender, interest, age, and engagement.

Ultimately, you might just ask your audience for the collaborator. Ask them who they also like watching, or you can do the work yourself. Check out the channels of your audiences and look for the connection.

Improving the Performance of Your Videos

If you have some videos that sit forgotten on your Channel or are looking for a way to bring more exposure to the ones that are performing with mediocre success, there are some ultimate strategies that can help you boost the way your videos perform on YouTube.

Here are the 4 secrets for enhanced YouTube performance:

#1: Monitoring Your Target Audience

The biggest reason why your videos do not result in success is perhaps the fact that you are not providing solutions to the issues that your audience have. The first thing you need to do is to monitor the concerns that your audience has in order to make sure that your videos actually address these topics. There are some incredible tools that are specially designed for the audience listening, in order to improve customer experience. Some of the best tools for that purpose are https://sproutsocial.com/ and https://hootsuite.com/.

#2: Have Your Signature Production Style Ready

Having the right content created to address your audience issues is probably the most important step, however, it will not bring you any success if you fail to deliver the content the right way. Your videos need to be compelling, engaging, and most importantly, of high-quality. You don't necessarily have to go all crazy with expensive, professional equipment, but a shaky camera may sentence your video to a lifetime of loneliness on YouTube. Here are the most important things you need to consider when making the video:

- Have an eye-catching title

- Craft an engaging narrative

- Edit your video for success

- Focus on delivering value to your customers

- End with a call-to-action

#3: Increase the Discoverability with Creator Studio

Your video may be slow in performance due to the fact that they (as well as your channel) are not optimized properly. How can you possibly expect thousands of likes if your audience cannot find your videos in the search results easily? In order to improve your video's performance, increasing their visibility is a hugely important step.

Within your Creator Studio, you will find many optimization options that you need to take care of, such as: adding a custom thumbnail, optimizing your title with relevant keywords, including brief summaries of the videos (again with relevant keywords), provide URLs that will lead your customers to your website or other social media platforms, adding tags to help people find your video better, adding a comprehensive transcript, etc.

All of these will help you make your video more discoverable. Just make sure to hit **'Save Changes'** when you're done, and your audience will be provided with the chance to discover your videos easily.

#4: Promote Your Channel on Social Media

This is a no-brainer, really. The more you promote your channel on other social media platforms, as well as your blog, the more people will discover your YouTube videos. It's as simple as that, and yet, most businesses fail to do this the right way.

While simply posting URLs that lead to your YouTube channel on Facebook will bring some exposure, that doesn't necessarily mean that you will get more views and improve the overall performance of your videos. In order to boost how your videos perform, you need to promote them where the audience will have the best chance of seeing them.

By default, this should mean promoting on the social media platform that your business prioritizes, however, there is more to it.

The best tactic is to check Google Analytics, not only to see which platform your audience uses the most, but to also do a split testing in order to determine which type of messaging they prefer. This will help you promote the right kind of videos to the right people in the way that they will appreciate the most.

When trying to improve the performance of your videos, keep in mind that the most important metric is the time watched, not the number of views. The more customers watch your video through to the end, the higher your rank on YouTube. These performance tips will help you improve your watch time, so make sure that each of your videos, as well as your channel is successfully optimized.

Generating Leads with YouTube

YouTube has an enormous lead potential, and yet, only a tiny portion of the small businesses actually have a channel there. That should encourage you to get more creative and start generating leads, before the rest of your competition realizes what they are missing out on and decides to tap into the golden potential.

Here are three tactics that will help you generate more views for your videos, drive traffic from your website, and increase the number of subscribers for your channel.

Driving Traffic with YouTube Cards

YouTube cards are the perfect trick up the marketer's sleeve, as they allow even further engagement on the uploaded videos. By adding a simple card on your video, you add a call-to-action to your content which will most likely provide you with additional interactivity. The links will direct the viewers where you want them to go and push them to take action and further engage.

Since this option was mainly created for the mobile users, it works seamlessly on all devices. That being said, you get the opportunity to send even those people that are watching your video via their mobile app, to your website.

How do YouTube cards work? When you add your card to your video, there will be a teaser window in the top right corner of your video. The teaser will be active for 5 seconds, meaning that the viewer has only 5 seconds to click on it, for the card to be revealed. If the viewer does not click on the teaser, in place of the card, the 'i' sign will appear.

You can easily add YouTube cards. The only thing you need to do is go to your **'Video Manager'** and find which video you want to add the card to. Open the drop-down menu found next to 'Edit' that is below your video, and click on **'Cards'**. Then go to **'Add Card'** and choose the type of card you wish to add (a link, video, channel, poll, or playlist) and click on **'Create'**. After selecting, you get to customize the card by, for instance, adding the URL for your Link card. Once you're all set, click on **'Create Card'**.

Now, all you have to do is to decide the spot where you want your card to be shown on your video. You can just drag the marker below the video to the spot where you want your card to appear.

Keep in mind that you will have the option to use additional cards, as well. However, if thinking about this option, you need to consider these:

- Your cards must be spaced out, so your viewers don't get too distracted. Otherwise, they might just click on something else from the recommendation sidebar.

- Even though adding multiple card may seem like a great way to encourage engagement, too many cards will most likely putt viewers off. Never use more than 3 cards for a higher rate of click-through.

- Do not use arrows that point to your cards. Not all devices show the videos the same way, and you might end up with an arrow that points in a totally different spot on the video, which let's face it, will look super spammy.

<u>Introducing Your Landing Pages with End Screens</u>

Adding an end screen to your video means ending with a call-to-action. Whether you want to prompt your viewers to subscribe to your channel, like your Facebook Page, or check out some more videos, end screens are the best way for you to achieve your goal.

To add end screens, just go to **'Video Manager'** and find the specific video you wish to add an end screen to. From the drop-down menu below your video, click on **'End Screens & Annotations'.** Make sure that the 'End Screen' tab is the one that's selected before you continue.

Important: You will be allowed to create an end screen only if your video is longer than 25 seconds, as the end screen is placed in the final five to twenty seconds of the video.

To create an end screen, you have three options to choose from:

1. The first option is to choose <u>a ready template</u> for your end screen. These predefined themes have all of the elements that an end screen should have, and are a very convenient way for YouTubers to ask for more engagement. Just choose the one that you find to be the most attractive, and then further customize it to fit your needs.

2. The second option is to make your <u>end screen from scratch</u>. This obviously requires a lot more work than the previous option, but it is also the best way to ensure that your brand will be presented in the best way possible. Here is where you can get really creative (or hire someone else to do it for you) and find the elements that will suit your video the most. To add an element, just click **'Add Element'** select the ones you want to add (you are allowed 4 elements max), fill in the details, and then finish by clicking **'Create Element'**. When selecting the elements, keep in mind that one of them has to be a video (or a playlist).

3. The third option is to simply <u>import the end screen from another video</u> of yours. If some of your videos include end screens, you can easily import one from there. Just click on **'Import from Video'** and then

select the posted video. In the end, you will also have the option to edit the selected elements.

Generate Leads via Search

When it comes to YouTube (and Google in general) searches, the contextual keyword phrases are, without a shred of doubt, at the core of the queries. With that in mind, you can just imagine how detailed and well-explained description can help you rank high, not only on YouTube but on web searches as well.

Obviously, the longer your description is the higher your chance for getting discovered. However, long descriptions are more than just a bunch of long-tail keywords. When writing your video descriptions, make sure to make it as in-depth as possible, and include many different variations of your relevant keywords. By doing so, you may come up with something new and catch attention for some phrases that you didn't even use, which is pretty amazing.

While lengthy descriptions are great for recognition, what's more important is that first couple of lines that are shown without clicking on the 'Show More' button. Also, make sure to include the URL to your website so you can drive traffic there as well. But don't just copy and paste it. It is recommended that you add a UTM parameter to the link so you can track the clicks generated by the video. To make the link clickable, include **https://** so your viewers can be redirected to your website with a single click.

Marketing on Instagram

Even if your photos are of high quality and your posts are visually stunning, that alone will not bring you marketing success on Instagram. Just like with any other platform, promoting your brand on Instagram requires putting in a lot of work and knowing some techniques that will make you really stand out and slay the competition.

If your Instagram account is picture pretty but you still struggle to spread awareness and get some engagement from your followers, it is obvious that you need to find some new techniques to boost your following and get some interaction started. Read on to see what you can do to improve your Instagram marketing.

Taking Advantage of Instagram Stories

Most small businesses rely on posting pictures, overwhelming the audience with hashtags, and then waiting for someone to respond. Which is great, if you have been doing that for a while and already have an established audience. But if you are a small fish hoping to swim with the big sharks, then you need some big tactics in order to survive. Taking advantage of Instagram stories is one of those tips.

Although they are considered to be the new kid on the block – arrived in 2017 – Instagram Stories play a huge part in the marketing strategies of many businesses. Thanks to their ephemeral nature, these posts have really made a breakthrough.

So, what is Instagram Stories? Instagram Stories is a feature on Instagram that allows you to post images and videos that will remain visible on your account for up to hours. After that, they simply vanish into thin air. Whether you are planning to post a fun and upbeat short video or a business-focused photo, your business can definitely find value in this feature.

How Often is Too Often?

The greatest fact about this feature is that it will not get your account penalized for posting too often. In fact, you can post as many stories as you like on a daily basis. And because of the fact that these posts live only one day (as long as they are not highlighted, of course), they are shown in chronological order and there aren't any priorities on the feed. However, that doesn't mean that these posts are any less valuable than the regular ones. They are just as affected by the Instagram algorithm as any other post. However, with Instagram Stories, the frequency of your posts doesn't affect the number of people that will see the stories.

But, keep in mind that if you post too often you might look a bit spammy, and your followers may even decide to mute the posts from your account. There isn't really a secret to how often you should post. Keep in mind that posting too often requires a lot of time, effort, and management involved. While some companies have higher engagement if they post 10 stories per day, only you can decide whether you have that connection with your audience or not. Just know that once you establish the frequency of your stories, your followers will expect a continuance.

If you are a small business just getting into the waters of Instagram marketing, don't go overboard with this feature. Posting one story a day (or only a couple per week) may be the optimal frequency for achieving the goal of your business.

Posting Stories for Your Business

Just like with your regular Instagram posts, the Instagram Stories should also be engaging, informational, appealing, and promotional. But unlike with regular posting, the quality standard for Instagram Stories is pretty low. This gives you the opportunity to show your audience the raw, unpolished side of your business. It is also allowed to be a bit more relaxed or even goofy.

Many businesses have managed to drive engagement with this more natural side of promoting their brand. Using Instagram Stories is an essential tactic for many, so make sure to make it a part of your marketing strategy. Don't have any ideas on how to start your Story? Here are the most popular ways that businesses use this amazing feature for:

Promote Your Products or Services

The best thing about Instagram Stories is that it allows the audience to get a real and more natural feeling about your products or services. With a single 'tap', you can post a raw photo of your product that your customers will appreciate. Have a new product launched recently? Fill your Stories with different-angle photos of the product, photos of people using that product, or photos of your product in various environments. Just don't forget the call-to-action at the end, and you see how engaged your followers can be.

Behind the Scenes Look

To bring more authenticity to your content and invite your customers to take a peek at what's going on in your company during business hours, posting some behind-the-scenes content is probably the best way to achieve that. This is perfect for business of all sizes, as well. For instance, your small pastry shop can post a photo of your new pie and another behind-the-scenes photo of your employee making the pie. Or a large real estate company could take its audience around a new property that they have recently announced. There are endless possibilities of how this feature can be used.

Build an Engaged Community

Instagram Stories are usually posted with the purpose to encourage more followers to participate in the conversation. And since these posts are deleted from your feed after 24 hours, you shouldn't think too much about the lighting, the camera position, or about polishing the photo. This is the perfect chance for you to show your relaxed side and post light-hearted content that will make your follower's day and inspire them to become engaged.

People like honesty and genuineness. Showing them this side of yours by, for example, posting a short video of your team dancing to their favorite tune while out for a post-work drink, may be just the thing your brand needs to keep your followers coming back for more.

Run a Takeover

An Instagram Story takeover means having segments with regular guests to bring some more consistency to your business Instagram account. You can do this with members of your team, or you can even partner up with another business to swap your stories for a day. This will bring variety to your content and inspire your audience to engage with your posts.

Features to Use

To use Instagram Stories as a part of the marketing strategy of your business, there are some features that you can make use of in order to present your brand in the best light, and get the most engagement from your followers.

Location and Hashtag Stickers

When the stickers were first introduced in 2017, they were nothing but a fun way to share your stories with your followers. But thanks to the new functionalities that Instagram has added, stickers are now as useful as they are fun, which makes them perfect for businesses to use when sharing a rawer side of their brand with the audience. The best of these functionalities are the ability to search Instagram Stories by hashtag and location.

Adding a Location

Adding a location sticker to your Instagram Stories can be of huge importance for your business, because by searching Instagram Stories by location in the Explore page, users can come across your Instagram Story and may even discover your brand that way.

To add a location, tap the sticker button and click on the **'Location'** option. A list of nearby locations will appear. Select the right one, and add your post. By tapping on the sticker, you can customize it by changing its color, etc.

Adding a Hashtag

Adding a hashtag to your Instagram Stories is just as simple. Just tap on the hashtag sticker, write your hashtag, and that's it.

You can easily resize these stickers by expanding or pinching with two fingers.

Important: If you want your Stories to be seen by the public, make sure to set your account to Public. That way, when a user tags a hashtag in their Stories, or searches Instagram Stories by location, your Stories will come up.

Links

Adding clickable links to your Instagram Stories is a pretty big deal, as it will allow you to drive traffic to your website, YouTube channel, other social media platforms or another landing page that is relevant for your business.

Adding a Link

To add a link, you first have to have your video or photo taken. Next, click on the 'link' button at the top. You will be taken to a page where you will be prompted to enter (or paste) the URL to your landing page. When you're all set, just click **'done'** and that's it.

Adding a Call-to-Action

Keep in mind that your link will not be visible on the photo or video unless your followers swipe up the **'see more'** button. That being said, you can see how having this button will not be enough to entice your audience to click it and reveal the link.

Since the link button isn't as obvious as you'd want it to be, you have to let your audience know that they are supposed to take an action. Adding a call-to-action is the best way to do it. Call your users out by using appealing text or even arrow to get their attention.

Tagging

Tagging can also be a great way for you to redirect your followers to another landing page, and it can be your powerful weapon for driving traffic.

For instance, if you are running a contest, an influencer campaign, or even if you are planning a takeover, tagging other accounts can be of great importance for your overall marketing strategy.

Polls

Customers love feeling important, so asking their opinion on something can make them feel more valuable and will, in turn, result in increased engagement on their side. Including poll questions is a great way for you to include your customers in making decisions.

For instance, post an Instagram Story with a photo of two of your newest products, and create a poll where your audience can vote to let you know which product they want to see on discount first, or something of that sort.

To add your polls, take a photo or video, open the **'Stickers'** menu and click on the **'Poll'** sticker. Next, simply write your question and customize the choices. Now, post your story and wait to hear what your followers think.

Whether it is to see what your customers think of a certain product, crowdsource new ideas, or simply to post fun content for the sake of entertainment, the poll sticker gives your business many beneficial choices for your marketing strategy.

Countdown Stickers

Countdown stickers are a great way for you to emphasize the importance of taking an action in regard to an upcoming sale or discount that is about to end. Also great for announcing new product launches, adding a sticker that counts the remaining time is a perfect opportunity for you to send your customers a reminder in order to generate more results.

To add a countdown sticker, just tap the **'Stickers'** button, select the **'Countdown'** option, and add the details for your countdown.

<u>Instagram Stories Highlights</u>

As previously mentioned, highlighting Instagram Stories means giving your Story a permanent life that will not be deleted after 24 hours. Instagram Stories Highlights are an incredibly valuable feature that will allow your business to curate your content easily, in order to showcase those photos or videos that you want your audience to see first.

The best thing about these Highlights is that you can group them together by a topic or a theme, and make them a permanent part of your feed; until you decide to delete them, of course.

The Instagram Stories Highlights are displayed right under your bio and act as completely stand-alone Stories when a user clicks on them to view.

To add an Instagram Story Highlight, go to your profile and click on the **'Story Highlights'** found under your bio. Tap the **'+'** button, select the Story you wish to highlight, and click **'Next'**. Then you can simply choose a cover photo for your story and give it a name. Click **'Add'** or **'Done'** (depending on your device), and voila. Your story has now a permanent spot on your feed.

Driving the Best Results with Carousel Posts

Since they first appeared in mid-2017, carousel posts have really made a difference in the way in which businesses attract their audience. Much more versatile than regular Instagram photo posts, carousel posts allow you to promote product lines in a better, much appealing light. This feature of combining multiple images or videos in a single Insta post will provide your business with the opportunity to send your followers a much clearer marketing message.

Creating Carousel Posts

To create a carousel post, start by tapping the **'+'** sign, as you would normally do when adding an image. Once you do that, you will see a **'Create Multiple'** sign of stacked squares. Click on it. Scroll down your list of images or videos and select the ones you want to combine in a single post. You can select anywhere from 2 to 10 files. Click **'Next'**.

On the next screen that appears, you will have the option to **apply filters** and edit your images before posting. Keep in mind that any chosen filter will be applied to all of the selected images for the post. To edit the images individually, just tap on the image that you wish to apply filters to and choose the **edit** option. Once you are done, click on **'Done'**. If you want to reorder your images, just tap and hold the image you wish to change the order of, and then drag it to the desired spot.

After selecting and editing your images, you will be prompted to add your caption, just as you would in a regular post. And that's it. Just tap the **'Share'** button and your carousel post can be shared with your audience.

You can share portrait, landscape, and square formats in carousel posts, however, you are allowed to choose only one photo format per post.

The Uses

There are many different ways in which your business can turn these carousels posts to its advantage. These are some of the best uses that businesses have found multi-image posts to be beneficial for:

New Product Line Launches

Whether you want to promote your new eyeshadow line or your pet care business, sharing several photos of your new photo line is the best way not only for attracting your followers to click on your post and check out the new products, but also perfect for making more sales.

Does your product come in different colors? Carousel posts would be the perfect way to let your audience know that there is the perfect shade for everyone.

Capturing Multiple Features

Have a new product that is multi-functional? The best way to show off its capabilities is to create a carousel post and include an image of each of its valuable features. For instance, if you are selling a cotton baby carrier that can be also used as a car seat cover, a nursing cover, or a cute poncho for the mom, the best promoting strategy would be to capture all of these functions and combine it together in a single post. A short, fast-forwarded video of a mom transforming the carrier into its other functions would be the cherry on top.

Walking Through Step-by-Step Tutorials

The carousel post is perhaps best used when providing step-by-step tutorials of how something is done. For instance, if you want to share a recipe where the main ingredient is your organic coconut oil, this use will be your best strategy. Just divide the steps of the recipe into distinct sections, add an image (or a short video) for each of them, and then combine them into a single post to tickle the audience's taste buds and compel them to give it a try.

Behind-the-Scenes, How-It-Is-Made Photos

Insta Stories may be the perfect way to allow your followers to take a peek behind the scenes, carousel posts can also be a great way to share with your audience the making-of process of your product/service. Take a photo (or a short video) of each of the steps of the process of making your product, select them all for your carousel post, and let your audience see how your products are made.

Showcasing Before-And-After Sequences

This option works best if you are in the renovating or restoring business, and the concept here is pretty obvious. Share a photo of an old table from before, and then one of how the same table looks after your business has brought it back to life. But these sequences can have more meanings. Everyone can use this feature. Showcasing how your product works in real life can be one great way for this. And the best part? You can share up to 5 before-and-after sequences in a single post.

IGTV for Businesses

The moment that IGTV launched as the stand-alone video platform of Instagram, many businesses took the opportunity to take their Instagram marketing strategy to another level. And they were right. IGTV offers a new channel for your brand to promote itself, showcase your products and services, and grow your following. And the best thing about this is that, just like Insta Stories, IGTV is also a pretty relaxed space. You don't have to be obsessed with all the filters and polishing like you should be when sharing a high-class Instagram post. Think of IGTV as something between a regular post and Instagram Stories that can help you stretch the brand awareness even further.

Posting on IGTV

Posting on IGTV is pretty limitless. From product launches, how-to-tutorials, to sharing business info, so far, businesses have managed to gain success in many different ways on IGTV. The important thing – as with any other marketing strategy- is for you to be able to find a way to create value to your audience that will eventually result in value for your brand.

But first things first, before you can upload your content to IGTV you, obviously, need an IGTV account. So, download the IGTV app on your device, and sign up with your Instagram account. Then, click on the gear icon found in the upper right corner, and tap **'Create Channel'**.

Once your channel is created, you need to open it in order to upload content. To do so, click on your avatar from the main page. Then, click the '+' icon, and add your video to IGTV.

Keep in mind that if your video is not shown, it is probably because it is the wrong aspect ratio. For vertical videos, your aspect ratio should be a minimum 4:5 and a max of 9:16.

Next, simply add the title of your video and write a compelling description. Just like with YouTube videos, think about optimizing your IGTV content with relevant keywords. You can also add links, as your audience can be redirected to another landing page.

Finally, choose a thumbnail or add your own cover image. This image is what will be shown in the categories on IGTV, as well as up on your profile, so make sure it is visually compelling.

The aspect ratio for your cover photo should be 1:1.55 or 420 x 654 pixels.

2-Step Path to Success on IGTV

If you are already a pro in posting Instagram Stories, then beginning with IGTV shouldn't seem overwhelming or intimidating. Just think about IGTV as a simple step up from the Insta Stories. You can even use the same style and voice you use when sharing your Stories.

The only thing you need to consider here, is that IGTV, unlike Instagram Stories, means posting long-form content. That means that you will need some more time to shoot and edit your videos before actually publishing them. However, you can easily create a successful IGTV marketing strategy if you stick to these 2 golden rules:

#1: Be Comfortable with Vertical Videos

If editing video is not something you are comfortable doing, you will need some practice in order to post on IGTV. Why? Because unless you are shooting your video on your smartphone (most of them record vertically in 9:16 aspect ratio), you will need to edit the videos in post-production in order to get the aspect ratio right and be able to post on IGTV.

Lucky for you, you don't need to spend your money on expensive software or editing lessons. You can easily do this on your desktop. The first step you need to do is to download iMovie on your Mac desktop. Open it and create a new project. Rotate your video clip (if it is vertical) to avoid the tool adding black borders to the clip's sides, with the crop button. Then, edit your video as you see fit and save the file.

Don't forget to open the video in QuickTime before uploading it to your smartphone so you can rotate it back to being vertical again. Just go to '**Edit**' and rotate your video left or right.

Windows users can do the same using a tool like OpenShot, Movie Maker, or VideoPad.

Track the IGTV Analytics

IGTV is relatively new on Instagram, so it is still early for predicting how the audience responds to the uploaded content as well as for looking for certain patterns in their behavior. For that purpose, keeping a close eye on IGTV"s analytics is the best way to stay on top of things and determine which content needs tweaking and which yields the best results.

IGTV's analytics can be accessed directly from the uploaded video. Just below the likes, views, and comments of your video, you can see it's retention rate, which shows you just how many of the viewers stuck with the content all the way through. But that's not all. If you open the drop-down graph, you will see exactly when the viewers decided to swipe   away. This can be extremely beneficial as it is a great indicator of the performance of your videos. For instance, if most people decided to drop off after 15 minutes of watching, that can be a clear sign that your video shouldn't be that long. Having the analytics in mind, you can further edit or even reshot your videos in order to provide more value to your potential customers.

Your Influencer Marketing Strategy

Unless you have no social media account and aren't particularly interested in spending time online, chances are, you are pretty familiar with the term *influencer.* Influencers, as the name itself suggests, are those individuals who have managed to influence other people with their actions, position, knowledge, etc.

Influencers can be found throughout history, although when you hear this term today, it is unlikely that the topic is about Martin Luther King influencing with his civil right movement or Isaac

Newton with his invaluable scientific discoveries. Influencers, in the modern sense of the word, are social media users who have the power to affect (or change entirely) someone's purchase choice thanks to their established credibility in a specific industry.

So, what is *influencer marketing* and how does it work? Influencer marketing is an inexpensive and highly effective strategy to grow your business on social media. It generally includes a brand partnering up with a popular Instagrammer (influencer) with the purpose of promoting their products/services. The influencer already has a large audience, and by promoting the brand's products, his/her followers will be persuaded to make a purchase. It's a simple trick that seems to be working like a charm.

Influencer marketing is a very popular strategy for spreading brand awareness and growing your following, as it breaks the traditional barriers of marketing and allows you to reach your customers through a source that they actually trust. So, when an influencer posts a picture of them trying a certain product or service, it doesn't seem as staged as having a celebrity promoting your brand, for instance, but it comes across as if their audience received a genuine recommendation from a friend.

Despite the fact that you can implement an Influencer Marketing strategy on almost any social media platform, it is highly recommended to give this journey a try on Instagram, as it is the best platform for social action.

Did you know? 67% of all marketers are already promoting their brand with influencers.

The Cost

Now that I've managed to tickle your imagination and got you thinking about giving Instagram Influencer Marketing a try, you must be wondering what that means for your budget. Influencer Marketing, just like the influencers themselves, really comes in all sizes. So, you can only imagine how the marketing rates vary. If you are looking to find an influencer who has over 100k followers, obviously, you have to be ready to pay a pretty substantial price. According to a 2018 report, some influencers even charge from $5000 to $10000 per one post. However, the common range is from $250 to $1000.

Keep in mind, though, that there are many factors that can determine the price of Influencer Marketing, and in the end, influencers with huge following may not even bring success to your business.

Micro-Influencer Marketing

If you are thinking about giving up on the idea of Influencer Marketing because of your tight budget, wait before you skip to the next chapter. To cash in on the influencer trend, you don't necessarily need to have thousands of dollars to spend. For your business, Micro-Influencer Marketing may be just what you need to reach to potential customers.

Micro influencers are those influencers who don't have hundreds of thousands of followers on their Instagram account, but they do have a smaller (micro) audience that is super engaged.

Now, micro can be anywhere from 1,000 to 100,000 followers. It all comes down to what kind of audience you want to be introduced to and what you are looking from an influencer.

The great thing about these micro-influencers is that unlike regular Instagram influencers who have attained a celebrity-like status, micro-influencers, come across as regular customers who can be super relatable and easy to trust. This is a great perk for small businesses as these influencers usually retain a higher engagement rate.

So, which type of influencer would be a better fit for your business? A celebrity-like individual who lives an almost-fairytale-like life, or a popular but trustworthy person who can recommend your products to about 5,000-15,000 people, giving a more genuine consumer message?

Want to know the best part about Micro-Influencer marketing? Most of these influencers do not promote products or services for money, but for free samples and gifts. Some of them also charge based on the leads or the sales that the sponsored post results in. It all depends on your marketing goal, your budget, and what you are trying to get out of this marketing strategy.

Why Your Business Needs It

With most businesses taking advantage of this popular marketing strategy, you really cannot afford to pass on an opportunity like this. If you're still wondering whether your business really needs this, let me tell you – it most certainly does. Instagram Influencer Marketing can be a real game-changer for your brand and will help your business row on many levels:

Increasing Brand Awareness

If you are a relatively new business, then your whole strategy should be based on building brand awareness in these initial stages. Teaming up with an influencer who already has the power to persuade their loyal fanbase what's good and what's not, can be a great way to present your products/services to a larger group of people. Think about it. If you team up with 3 influencers and have each of them post about a certain product of yours, you will have way more people looking at your products than you could have with 300 posts shared on your account.

Driving Sales

Influencer marketing is a great opportunity for you to drive more sales. Why? Because these influencers already have an engaged audience that is influenced by the things they do and want to buy the products they use. If played the right way, this can turn out to be the only marketing strategy you'll ever need. Take the watch company Daniel Wellington for an example. They solely depend on Instagram Influencer Marketing in order to drive sales. In 4 years, they have managed to achieve annual revenue of an incredible $220, mostly thanks to this Instagram marketing strategy.

How? Instead of simply spreading brand awareness, they were more concerned with driving more sales. They offered each influencer a free watch for a sponsored post. The influencers, then, gave a discount of 10-20 percent through a limited promotional code, to those followers who wanted to buy a watch. This worked great for both sides because the influencers were not just posting an advertisement, but they were also providing value to their followers by giving them a really cool discount.

Building Excitement for New Launches

What better way to get people excited about a new launch than having a popular Instagrammer promoting it? The ultimate strategy here is to offer influencers free products that are yet to be launched that they should promote on Instagram (and get to keep, of course). That way you will not only market your products/services before they even hit the stores, but also position them as something cool through the excitement that the influencer is about to share with their fans.

Encouraging the Use of Your Branded Hashtag

If you have a branded hashtag and you want to get more people to use, then turning to an influencer for help can be just the thing you need. By having the influencer post with your #hashtag, their audience will be introduced to it and encouraged to jump on that bandwagon and use it in their posts, too. This will eventually result not only in increasing brand awareness but driving more traffic and sales as well.

Finding the Right Influencers for Your Brand

Now, to the trickier part. How do you actually find the right Instagrammer so that your business can benefit from their influence? Whatever your goal, the three things that you need to check before contacting an influencer are:

#1: Their Engagement

If an influencer has a lot of engagement, it means that their influence is pretty strong, and their followers are paying attention to their posts. Check their profile and see how their posts are performing. If the engagement rate is somewhere between 2 and 4%, that means that they have a solid audience who is engagement. A rate of 4 to 6 percent is excellent, while posts with an engagement rate higher than 15 or 20% are considered to be viral.

#2: The Quality of their Audience

If you are selling healthy and organic drinks and smoothies, it is obvious that you'd want to partner up with an influencer whose audience is interested in weight-loss, healthy living, nutrition, regular exercise, etc. Your influencer should have a following that is similar to your ideal audience, in order for your Instagram Influencer Marketing campaign to be successful.

#3: The Number of Followers

Okay, the number of followers isn't necessarily the best metric to look at, however, in some cases, teaming up with huge influencers can be a great strategy if you want to let the world know your brand exists. Just keep in mind that, in most cases, the rate of engagement decreases as the number of followers grows.

Finding the perfect influencer for your brand can be a bit of a challenge, but the most important thing is to be sure just what you are looking for. For instance, if you have a goal to just spread brand awareness, the important metrics to look for in an influencer would be traffic and reach. However, if you want to increase your engagement rate, then teaming up with a micro-influencer who has a smaller but more engaged audience would be the right tactic.

And if you are wondering what your approach should be like, that depends solely on you. What are you ready to offer and what is your budget? Craft a good and appealing proposal before actually contacting the influencer. You can offer a flat rate, a price per sale, free products, a very generous discount, whatever you think it's best for your brand.

Marketing on Twitter

Although Twitter has gained the reputation for being the noisy, microblogging site, it can actually be a great marketing tool for businesses of all sizes. But with over 500 million Tweets being sent each day, you can see that getting the right kind of attention in the middle of all that noise can be tricky.

If you've already started your Twitter marketing journey, chances are, you're already well aware that being so communication-oriented, Twitter is a social media platform that deserves a somewhat more customized marketing strategy. In order for you to be able to get through to your audience on the busiest network, this chapter will provide you with some tips and tricks for your business to succeed.

Promoting in 280 Characters

When Twitter decided to make the change from 140 to allowing 280 characters per post, that was probably the biggest social media shift since the transformation that Facebook made to its news feed a few years back.

But even though that it's doubled in size and may seem like a lot, once you start typing with the purpose of promoting your product in the best way possible, you will see that you cannot fit everything you want to say. And compared to the thousands of characters allowed on Facebook, Twitter can seem quite frustrating at times.

Here are some tips on how to make the most out of this character limit, and how to make your brand's Tweets engaging:

Don't Use Shortened Words – Many people use shortened words (think *u* instead of *you*, or *4* instead of *for*, etc.) to be able to fit their thoughts into the 280-character limit. But while this may seem like a smart thing, keep in mind that abbreviations give an unprofessional feeling. Your sentences should be clear. If your followers cannot read and understand the sentence at first glance, you will definitely lose them.

Use Characters – You may come across as unprofessional if you spell the word *great* as *gr8*, but using allowed characters is totally approved. Why waste your characters to say *percent*, when % will say the same thing with a single character?

Use Shorter Words Instead – Instead of cutting your word short, use their shorter counterparts instead. For instance, if you want to say *enormous*, stick to its shorter synonym *big* to explain the same thing in fewer characters. Just be sure to use the right words, as not all synonyms send the same message.

Make Every Word Count – Avoid using filler words. Make sure that every word you type in makes an impact and shows and actions, and avoid empty words such as *that.*

Do Not Skip on Punctuation - Do not be tempted to skip the comma or the period for the sake of the character count. Punctuation matters and run-on promotions are definitely not going to attract your audience.

Get to the Point - Try not to mince your words but get right to the point. This will not only save you a lot of characters but posting clear sentences attract people's attention more.

Try not to Break Up Your Tweets – Dividing your Tweets in order to continue your thought may be the only way in which you can completely make your point, but keep in mind that not everyone will see both of your Tweets. Many of your followers may actually end up getting confused and not understand what it is that you're talking about.

Twitter Advanced Search for Getting More Leads

Lead generation is of incredible value for any business, as it is all about collecting info from potential customers and passing them onto your team, in order to incorporate the features your customers are looking for into your products/services with the purpose of driving more sales.

However, with over 6,000 tweets that happen per second, you can see how barraging through the Twitter clutter can be overwhelming. Finding specific info in the middle of all that noise can be next to impossible. For that purpose, Twitter has provided us with a great built-in tool called the *Advanced Search* that will save you tons hours of time and wasted energy.

If you want to get the most out of this tool for the sake of your brand's lead generation goals, follow the next few tips:

Explore Keywords and Hashtags

The most obvious way to use the Advanced Search is for exploring keywords and hashtags that are relevant for your business. By doing so, you will be able to reveal an entire community of people who are talking about your field. For instance, if you are a healthy drinks company, you would probably want to explore keywords such as *diet* or hashtags like *#weightloss* or *#health*. This will help you to follow real-time conversations that are centered around a certain topic that is related to your business.

Target Your Searches by Location

Whether you have a local thrift shop or are running an international business, it is always the best strategy to connect with your audience on a local level. By listening to the conversations of your potential customers from a specific location, you will be able to gather solid info about what they're buying habits are. Why? Because people in Los Angeles and Dallas may be talking about different needs. Narrowing your search by location will help you make a more continuous relationship with your customers.

Search by Sentiment

Once you start using the Advanced Search option, you will see that there are many different filters that can be applied to your searches, which is of great value when you are looking for high-class leads. One of the best options available is *searching by sentiment.*

Searching by sentiment will allow you to refine your search and check out only the positive things that are said about your business, or the other way around. This can be of huge importance if you are looking to reach out to an ambassador of your brand, as you are more likely to find the most loyal customers when you are only going through the positives.

But searching only for the negatives can also lead to growing your success. By determining what the main complaints of your customers are, you will be able to pinpoint exactly what needs to be modified in order to decrease the bad experiences associated with your brand.

Answering Questions

Similarly to searching by sentiment, you can also use the Advanced Search tool to look for questions. The question filter will help you find specific concerns or issues that Twitter users have within your field. Finding the right questions that you can give your answer to will help you reach out to more customers. You just need to explore the types of questions that people ask – whether about your business in particular or another related subject – and position your brand as the main authority of that particular subject. This will result in more followers, and eventually, more paid customers.

Hosting a Twitter Chat

A *Twitter Chat* is the place where Twitter members who share similar interests, come together at a previously determined time in order to communicate and share their thoughts on a specific topic with the use of a designated hashtag for every contributed tweet. There is a host (or a moderator) who is in charge of asking the questions to the participants, and it is the one who encourages the interaction. Twitter chats last about an hour on average.

Why You Should Participate

A Twitter Chat can be a very powerful tool for the marketer. When hosted regularly (once a week), Twitter Chats can provide your brand with the chance to connect with your community in a better way. By discussing issues that everyone is affected by, you can share tips and ideas with your community, and grow your circle and strengthen the connection with your audience in return.

Here is what your brand can get out of hosting a Twitter Chat:

- You get to create brand awareness by having a strong, engaging presence

- You can get people talking about you with your hashtag

- Your audience may have a good time and share the chat with others

- You will create a conversation among people with similar interests

- By having your hashtag appear on the stream, it may attract other people and you may end up with more followers

- You can meet other professionals, collaborators, and other people that can be valuable to your business

- You will help people learn about your community

Finding the Right #Hashtag

The hashtag is the single most important part of Twitter posts. It is a relevant word preceded by '#' that categorizes messages or helps users search for tweets. If you are already active on Twitter, then you probably know what hashtags mean for this network.

The hashtag in the Twitter Chat has the same meaning. It stands for the name of the chat, and it is mentioned in every Tweet, It is also how users can discover your chat.

You may think that coming up with a hashtag is simple, but the truth is, this is the hardest part. Why? Because there already are tons of chats out on Twitter already, and you need to come up with one that hasn't been used. It also has to be short (since it has to be mentioned in every Tweet), but also simple and clear.

The hashtag is what can make or break your chat, so choose wisely. The most popular chats are the ones that use the most obvious chats. For instance, *#blogchat* is a chat about bloggers.

The first part of the hashtag is usually the brand's name, and the end of the hashtag, the word *chat* is added so that users know what the hashtag is about. Your hashtag has to reflect your brand and has to be unique. For instance, if you're a wooden toy manufacturer, your hashtag may be *#woodentoyschat* or *#thenameofyourbrandchat* or whatever makes your chat stand out and helps people discover it.

Scheduling Your Chat

Your Twitter Chat must have a scheduled time and date in order for users to know when to partake. But you cannot simply set the time that works for you without making some prior considerations first. The most important thing that you need to think about is when your audience will actually be able to participate. For instance, you cannot choose to host the chat in the morning for Europe and expect to receive engagement from Pacific Time as well. If your audience is in different time zones, you need to find the perfect balance and choose the time that will work for the majority of your audience.

Also, don't forget to think about the time when your audience is most active on Twitter. This cannot be done without some trial and error, so feel free to experiment until you find the perfect timing for your Twitter Chat.

Making a Plan

You will need to create a good plan in order to make your chat successful. The most common mistake that businesses make is they tend to make the topic too specialized and fail to receive participation from users that are outside of their niche. Of course, keep your topic brand-focused, but don't make it to boring to encourage other people to join.

Once you decide on the topic that the chat will focus on, get more specific and write down the details. What questions are you planning to ask? The general rule of a thumb is for the host to ask about 6 - 10 questions, but this, obviously, depends on your business and your preferences. Since the Twitter Chat has a Q&A format, your questions should be composed in a compelling and engaging way to get more answers from the participants.

Make sure to also have a few back-up questions prepared that you will be able to throw in depending on the direction of the chat. Make a plan, but don't be afraid to go with the flow. This will give your conversation a more natural course and will encourage your chatters to come back for more.

Finding the Guests

A Twitter Chat can be a great way for you to share your expertise and ask for feedback from your audience. But if your plan is to be at the heart of the conversation every time, things may get quite boring after a chat or two. For that purpose, bringing in guests who will share their thoughts is a great way for you to stay within your area of expertise and still reach new audiences.

So, take your time to do some research in order to find the movers and shakers in your field, and ask them to join you for a chat. Let them know how they can also benefit from the chat to avoid being turned down: they will get more visibility, they will be able to promote themselves and their work, share some stats with them to prove your point, etc.

Hosting with Success

As a great host, you will need a certain chat format to stick to. If you are planning to run a 60-minute chat, try this format to yield the best results:

#1: Welcome Community Members

Welcome your community members and everyone who wishes to participate at the beginning of your chat. Ask them all to introduce themselves and share a few details. Allow them about 3 minutes for this.

#2: Introduce the Format of the Chat

Most chats are prefaced with the first question as Q1. The users will respond with A1 as the first answer, and so on. This is a great way to avoid getting confused and know exactly which question a certain answer refers to.

When asking questions to your guests, do not forget to use the '@' sign when replying. For instance, *@yourguest'sname, why do you think that is?*

#3: Retweet

Make sure to retweet your guest's answers, as well as your own questions. Also, check out the responses that are being shared by your community the most, and make sure to retweet those, too.

#4: Plan for Your Next Question

It's recommended to ask the next question not before 6 minutes and not longer than 10 minutes after starting the chat. The point is to plan your minutes wisely, so you have enough space not only to ask the questions, but also to respond.

#5: Let Your Guests Ask

If you have some time on your hands, allow your guests a couple of minutes to ask your guest some questions.

#6: Wrap It Up

About 2-3 minutes before the end, ask your guests if there is something they wish to end or promote.

#7: Sign Out!

End your chat by making your special announcements and reminding everybody of your next chat. If you already know who your guest will be, make sure to let your guests know.

Who Said What? If you are having a hard time keeping up with your guest's answers, you may want to seriously consider viewing your chat outside of Twitter. For instance, http://tweetchat.com/ is a great platform that allows you to only view the tweets for a particular hashtag, so this is a great opportunity to avoid getting confused by other tweets in your stream.

The Ultimate Dos and Don'ts of Twitter Marketing

You may think that your number one strategy should be making each and every one of your tweets about highlighting your products, but the line between successfully promoting and spamming is rather a thin one. The balance here is delicate, and if you try too hard to get people's attention, you might end up losing your existing followers. The beauty of Twitter – which other social media platforms lack of – is that it is the number one network for conversational promoting. That means that you get to promote your brand without even promoting it.

By being connected to the right people, talking to your audience the right way, and providing nothing but value (and a dash of entertainment, obviously) you will create a killer marketing strategy that will get you across the street from your goal.

Play your promoting Twitter game by these rules to avoid sounding overly promoting and provide content that your Twitter followers will want to talk about:

DO Follow the Right People

Most businesses make a lethal mistake by following as many people as they possibly can, but that will only lower your credibility and make you look like a fraud. Following a huge group of people hoping that you will receive follows in return leads to nothing more but cluttered stream that people will find hard to follow. If you want to receive the best level of engagement, make sure that you follow only those people that truly matter to your business and that will receive the most value from your contents.

DON'T Auto-Follow Your Followers

Be smart about your followers. Do not auto-follow everyone who becomes a fan of yours. Avoid using an auto-follow ap that will automatically make you a follower of your followers. Why? Because those profiles that auto-follow their audience are easy to spot thanks to their follower/following ration. Such a disbalance will present you s a spammer, which may cost you many followers.

DO Use the Right Keywords

Thorough keyword research will show you which phrases your business is most likely to benefit from by mentioning them in the tweets. Make sure to use your keywords wisely in order to improve your Twitter's visibility.

DON'T Spam People Who Are Talking about These Keywords

Slapping people with links to discounts or promotional codes whenever you hear the name of your product will not drive more sales. Quite the contrary. People on Twitter hate being bothered, so make sure not to come out of the woodwork promoting your brand whenever a user uses a relevant keyword. The keywords should be mainly used as suggestions and guides, not a reason for you to hit a sales pitch to every Twitter user who is interested in the relevant keywords.

DO Talk about Your Brand

Sure, Twitter may be all about the conversation, but don't forget why you're there. Take the time to talk about your brand and introduce your audience with the new launches, features, updates, and other important business-related stuff that your followers can benefit from.

DON'T Talk Only about Your Brand

The key to running a successful Twitter campaign is to find the perfect balance between promoting your brand and communicating with your followers. Of course, this ratio is not set in stone and is different for every business. Trial and error is ultimately the best tactic to find what works for you best, however, marketing experts say that the perfect ratio is 1-2 promotional tweets out of 10 tweets.

DO Find Interesting Topics to Talk about

Introducing appealing topics to discuss with your audience will increase their engagement and even bring you more followers. Go for a new topic each day. Try to find some news that is related to your business, or talk about some of your newest techniques, etc. Just make sure that the discussion will interest your followers.

DON'T Be Too Corporate

Keep in mind that your followers are not on Twitter to talk about your brand. Avoid sharing corporate content that will make you no fun to be around. You are allowed to share company business from time to time, but make sure to bring entertainment back to your Twitter. It's all about the balance.

Marketing on LinkedIn

What will make users mute your posts on other social media platforms and crown you as *boring* will help you establish your brand as an authority on LinkedIn. LinkedIn is the biggest B2B network where publishing press releases and important company info is not only expected but will also get you the right connections and help you grow a successful business.

LinkedIn usually gets a bump mainly because people don't really know how to use it. Since it is centered around business-related content and not holiday photos, many decide to write this platform off. But just because it seems harder to connect with people on LinkedIn, doesn't mean is not possible.

If you are a B2B business, then this is the platform you should definitely invest the most of your time and energy in. But if you think that LinkedIn is nothing more but a network where job seekers upload their resumes hoping to get employed, you cannot be more wrong. LinkedIn can be an invaluable marketing tool if used the right way.

So, don't give up on LinkedIn just yet if you don't know what to do with your company page. This chapter will teach you all there is to know about marketing your business on this platform.

Optimizing Your Page

You may have created your business page on LinkedIn with success, but that doesn't mean that your strategy will be successful. Your company page is the public listing of your company, both in the LinkedIn's on-site search, as well as on Google. In order to make sure that your page will be easy-to-find and at the top of the search results, you will have to optimize it first. Here are some optimization tips for better performance and generating more leads:

Check Your Company's Info

Check to see if your NAP (name, address, and phone number) is actually consistent with the info on other listings. By doing so you make sure that people can reach you easily. This may sound as too obvious, but you'd be surprise of the damage that a single dot or a wrong digit can do.

Use the Banner Image

Your banner image – best at 646 x 220 pixels – can be just the thing you need to define your brand and make it really stand out on LinkedIn. Of course, it is recommended to stay with your brand's recognition style and colors, however, add a little more value to your LinkedIn audience. For instance, have something like "Become Our Follower to Learn how to Manage Your Team" written, that will offer a tempting proposition to the LinkedIn users.

Use the Link Wisely

Most users add links on their business page that lead to their homepage. Don't waste precious space and opportunity to direct people to a better landing page and use this chance to capture emails or even send a personalized message to your visitors.

Link Your Profile to Your Page

Linking your personal LinkedIn profile to your business page can be of great value. Go to your personal page and click on **'Experiences'**. Under **'Company Name'**, add the name of your company.

Don't Shy Away from Keywords

Just like with any other social platform, the use of relevant keywords is also crucial for your marketing strategy on LinkedIn. Make sure to use the right phrases that are relevant for your business throughout the page, but pay close attention to how you're using them in your 'About' section.

Have Your Employees on Board

Nothing screams *healthy business* like having content employees. Make sure to encourage your team not only to like your company's LinkedIn page but also to share your content. There are no better brand ambassadors than the people that are employed by the business.

Promoting and Selling on LinkedIn

If you want to highlight initiatives or special products on LinkedIn, there is no better way to do it than by using *showcase pages.* Showcase pages are, in a way, similar to your business page. They are stand-alone pages where you can make your big announcements and introduce people with your newest product launches or services, announce special events, or any other kind of opportunity that your business may benefit from. Think of a showcase page as a valuable addition to your business page where you can share a particular part of your business and engage with your audience.

For instance, if your company has multiple smaller brands, you can use showcase pages and create a special place for each of your brands. Something like Facebook Groups, but in a much more specific, business-related way.

Businesses use showcase pages because they can:

Share Info about Their Brand. Unlike writing a short status update, showcase pages make it possible for you to share as much as info as you'd want your LinkedIn audience to be aware of.

Share Info only with Relevant People. People follow only those showcases that particularly interested. For instance, if someone is interested in one aspect of your business but not in something else that you do, they will most likely follow only the showcase that is relevant to them. This means that you will have a more targeted audience, and that you don't have to sell your brand as much as you should on your business page.

Increase Engagement. Having many showcase pages means having many opportunities for establishing communication with your well-educated LinkedIn audience.

Creating a Successful Showcase Page

Before even thinking about creating a Showcase Page, it is of crucial importance that you know that Showcase Pages cannot be simply unpublished. If you want to delete and completely deactivate the page, you have to contact LinkedIn and ask them to remove it. With that in mind, you need to pay close attention od why and how you are creating your showcase page.

A showcase page can only be created by the administrator of the company page. In order to do so, follow the next steps:

1. Go to your company page and open the drop-down menu that is found next to the **'Edit'** button. Select **'Create a Showcase Page'**.

2. Now, a Showcase Page pop-up window will appear. Click on the **'Get Started'** button.

3. Enter the relevant information like the name of your Showcase Page, and appoint an administrator for the page.

4. Click on **'Create Page'**. At this point, LinkedIn will show you what your page will look like. If you are not happy with the look, make some changes. If it looks good, jump to the next step.

5. Finally, click on the **'Publish'** button and you're Showcase Page will go Live in no time.

Starting a LinkedIn Group

A LinkedIn Group is very different from your business page, personal LinkedIn profile, or even your showcase pages. LinkedIn groups are not about promoting your brand nor about selling your products. At least not in the obvious sense of the word, that is. Groups are about having a place to discuss certain niche or topics with your community, in order to grow your audience and increase their engagement. So, you might not be able to sell your services there, but by learning about your audience, LinkedIn Groups provide you with the opportunity of actually improving the sales process.

Why Your Business Needs a LinkedIn Group

If you are wondering whether creating and managing a LinkedIn Group is worth your time and money, take a look at these benefits to see just what you can get out of these groups:

Establishing Expertise - If you are a B2B business owner, then a LinkedIn Group may be just what you need to establish your reputation as being one of the biggest experts in your industry. By taking a part in discussions, you get to show off with your knowledge.

Driving Traffic – By placing links that direct to your website or another sales page, you will get the chance to drive more traffic there.

Expanding Your Reach – By having a group where you will discuss certain topics with like-minded people, you will easily make new connections.

Understanding Your Community – Since you will be communicating with your community, you will have the chance to learn about their questions, concerns, thoughts, etc. first hand. This will create a great opportunity for you to shape your content and your services with the purpose of attracting new customers.

Sending Weekly Updates – Being the owner of a LinkedIn Group, you will get the chance to send weekly messages to everyone who follows your group. This can be a great way for you to make sure that your community is aware of the latest company information, product updates, new events, etc.

Setting Up Your Group

Your LinkedIn group can be set up in a jiffy. It will not take more than just a couple of minutes, and the process is pretty simple and straightforward. Just follow the next steps and you will have one up and running in no time:

1. Find **'Interests'** at the top of your page, click on it, and then hit **'Groups'** from the drop-down menu. The page with the Group Highlights will appear.

2. Select **'My Groups'** found at the top of the page.

3. Find **'Create a Group'** in the left sidebar and click on it.

4. Now, enter all of the relevant info about your group: the name of the group, description, summary, website URL, etc. Keep in mind that the relevant keywords play a huge role here as well, so make sure to be engaging and descriptive, but also tactical.

5. Next, upload your photo or log. This is optional, but highly recommended.

6. When creating your Group, you will have the option to choose whether you want it to be public or not. If you don't want the Group to be public, make sure that **'Unlisted'** is checked.

7. Accept the Terms of Service.

8. Finally, hit the **'Create Group'** button.

And that's it. Now, you are a proud owner of a LinkedIn Group.

Standard or Unlisted Group?

There are two options for your LinkedIn Group –
you can choose it to be *standard* or *unlisted.*

In a Standard LinkedIn Group:

- The discussions will be shown in Google's
  search results

- The members of the Group can invite other
  LinkedIn users to join

In an Unlisted LinkedIn Group:

- The discussions will not be shown in search
  engine results

- Only the members of the group will be able
  to see the discussions

- Only the Group's administrator can invite
  (and approve) users to join the group

- A padlock icon will be shown to indicated
  that the group is unlisted

So, all in all, a standard group is an open, public
group, and an unlisted group is closed, private
group. Choosing the right one for your business is
something that only you can do. They both have
their pros and cons, but ultimately, it all comes
down to what you are looking for.

For instance, an unlisted group may be a better option for you to control the membership, as well as to reduce spamming. However, these groups don't grow at the same pace as the standard ones do. Having an open group may be a better option if your business is new, as it will be visible for everyone to see and might help spread brand awareness.

Inviting Users to Join Your Group

The first thing that you need to do after successfully creating a LinkedIn Groups, is to find the group some members. To increase the membership of the group, you will have to invite others to join:

1. Click on **'Interests'** from the top of your page, and then choose **'My Groups'** from the drop-down menu.

2. Select your Group.

3. Click on **'Manage'** found at the upper right corner.

4. Choose **'Send Invitations'** from you're the left sidebar. A pre-written invitation will appear. Keep in mind that there is no way for you to customize the invitation, but you need to send it as is.

5. Click on **'In'** found next to the **'Connections'** text box, and select those people that you're connected with that you want to send the invitation to. Know that you will also have the option to invite other people to join, even if you are not connected to them. All you have to do is simply type their email address in the connection name box.

6. Finally, click on **'Send Invitations'**. The people you've invited will then get a notification at the upper right corner of their LinkedIn page or receive an email (if you've sent invitations to people who are not your connections on LinkedIn).

LinkedIn as a Content Platform

LinkedIn offers the opportunity for you the publish content in a long form. Even if you have (and successfully use) a website or a blog, publishing longer content on LinkedIn will not only help you reach a more professional social network, but will also throw many other benefits your way:

- Your posts will become visible on your personal profile. This will further promote your brand as anyone who clicks on your professional profile on LinkedIn will be able to check out the post published by your brand.

- People that are not connected to your business can also see your post which creates a huge opportunity for brand recognition and increasing your audience.

- LinkedIn users can follow your published content, even if they do not choose to follow you.

- Every one of your connections will be notified about the published post, which only increases the probability that the people you're connected to will see the post.

- The chances for engaging with other professionals are significantly received, as readers can also like and comment on your posts.

Creating Your First Post

Your post can be easily created from your LinkedIn home page in just a few steps:

1. Click on **'Home'** at the upper left corner of your LinkedIn Page.

2. Select **'Write an Article'** from the top of your page.

3. Enter your title in the title area.

4. In **'Write Here'**, write (or paste) the content that you wish to publish.

5. Finally, click on **'Publish'** from the upper right corner.

Keeping It Professional

Since LinkedIn is a network for career-oriented and professional people, it is only understandable that you cannot post your content in the same style as you write your Insta captions. When posting on LinkedIn, you have to do it in a professional tone that will attract the attention not only of your connections but other LinkedIn members as well. Here are some tips that will help you write a successful LinkedIn post in a professional manner:

Solve Problems. Keep in mind that people want to know about what you do in order to solve some issues that they are dealing with. Make sure that your content will answer questions and solve problems. Your readers will appreciate if you guide them and teach, not post fluff.

Give Advice. Many young professionals who want to try themselves in your industry will appreciate having advice from experts. What are the things you wish you knew when you were starting out? Share some tips and educate.

Keep it Up-to-the-Point. Really long content makes people lose interest. Your LinkedIn posts should be between 500 and 800 words, so make sure not to publish longer content.

Respond to Comments. Make sure to respond to every comment. Your readers will appreciate that you value their opinion which will most likely encourage them to share your content.

Be Careful with the Links. Links can be included in your post, but only if they are part of the discussion and make links. Don't just drop links out of the blue as it will look unprofessional and spammy.

Use Rich Media. Adding some visual elements to your post will make it much more appealing. On LinkedIn, it is allowed to use images, presentation from SlideShare, as well as embed YouTube videos.

Once your post is published, do not forget to promote it. Make sure that you share a link to your post on your other social media platforms in order to grow your connections, increase awareness, and let your audience know that you are always working on something new.

Tips for Getting More LinkedIn Followers

Getting more people to like your company page on LinkedIn can feel like an impossible thing to achieve. But while attracting new followers can be somewhat a challenge, it is indeed possible.

Growing your following on LinkedIn comes down to two things:

1. Promoting your page on other platforms

2. Implementing some strategies to attract more people

And while the first point requires some commitment and effort on your side, I can definitely help you with the latter. Here are the ultimate tips that will help you increase the number of your LinkedIn followers:

- Create a badge for your LinkedIn page that will be placed on your website or blog. You can use the LinkedIn Plugin Generator for this purpose https://developer.linkedin.com/plugins

- Post regularly. According to LinkedIn, the most successful pages are the ones that post at least 20 times a month, so make sure that you update your community on a regular basis.

- Make sure to use the LinkedIn share buttons with your posts in order to encourage your readers to share your content.

- Share job opportunities postings on your LinkedIn business page. This is one of the main things that attracts the eye of the LinkedIn members, so make sure to take care of that.

- Be informative with your posts. The most successful posts are the ones that share the best information, so make sure to keep your followers updated with latest company news, product development, upcoming events, etc.

- Post at the BEST TIMES in order to improve your visibility and get the most engagement, which will, in turn, lead to growing your following. The rule of a thumb is to publish after business hours and in the mornings for the highest engagement rate.

- Make sure to include a link to your business LinkedIn page in the bio of your guest posts.

Marketing on Pinterest

Sill think that only Facebook and Instagram are the marketing platforms worth investing in? Well, think again. Did you know that a Pin is a hundred times more spreadable than a Tweet? Or that Pins live way longer than Facebook posts? Or that if your business takes the right approach, it can show its customers how to use your products/services in the most visually stunning way possible?

If you were attracted by Pinterest before but failed to wow your customers with your boards and pins, do not despair. Just because you haven't managed to draw the right attention from Pinners, doesn't mean that your marketing campaign on Pinterest is a vain attempt. This chapter will show you what have you been doing wrong and how to improve your strategy for growing your brand on Pinterest.

Quality Pins for More Saves

Saves, or formerly known as *repins,* mean saving something that was already pinned by someone. The pins you create will have to attract people visually, in order to compel them to save them to their board. 80 percent of the content that is shared on Pinterest is Saves. The first tactic of your marketing campaign on Pinterest should be to abide by the 80/20 rule. What does that mean? That means that you should share 20% of your own content and save 80% of the things that have already been pinned. This is a huge marketing mistake that most small businesses make in the beginning, so make sure to save 4 other pins for every piece of content that you share on Pinterest.

But even though the larger chunk of your content on your board should be repins, you still have to figure out how to create and share your content in order to make other people save your Pins. After all, that is the whole point on Pinterest Marketing – getting people to save your content in order to promote your brand. And for that purpose, you need to focus on creating and sharing Pins of high quality.

<u>Writing Your Pins</u>

Even though Pinterest is considered to be a visual platform where a little attention is given to the captions and titles, the truth is, it is the description of your Pins that help people discover them in the first place. Think about it, if they are not actually typing something like *organic all-natural face cream* in the search bar, how on earth will your potential customers be able to find your face cream Pins?

Here is how you can write a compelling Pin:

Go for Longer Descriptions – Research shows that it is actually the Pins that have longer descriptions that actually get the most saves. So, if you want to get more repins and click-through rates, go slightly over 300 characters when describing your Pins.

Include a Call-to-Action – This is a no brainer. If you want your Pins to be saved, tell people to click through. Including a killer CTA in your description can really make a difference.

Use Keywords – Keep in mind that your audience finds your content by using keywords. Like *organic, all-natural, face cream.* Make sure to find the ones that are relevant for your Pins and incorporate them into your descriptions. Just make sure not to overdo it as your description has to make a sense.

Include a Link to your Website – Whether your website, blog, sales site, or another landing page, the point is to direct your audience where you want them to go with a clickable link.

Mention Others - When sharing someone else's content, be sure to thank them by mentioning them.

Only 75-100 characters of your description will be shown in the grid view of your Pin, so make sure to add the most important info at the beginning.

Things to Know about Hashtags:

Hashtags on Pinterest do not have the same meaning as they do on Twitter or Instagram. They will not help your Pins show in search results, nor will improve your visibility. Here, hashtags are used simply as a categorical symbol that you can add to your description in order to help other find similar things.

It's important to know that hashtags on Pinterest can actually have the contra effect sometimes. By having a hashtag that users can click on, you can actually take your potential Pinners away, without a point to return. If you end up using a hashtag, however, make it super unique.

Designing Your Pins

In order for your Pins to get saved, they need to be no less than visually stunning. But just because you need to add high-class imagery doesn't mean that you have to be a designer. Just follow the next three guidelines when creating your Pins, and repins are guaranteed:

Rely on Custom Imagery and Effective Colors

You may be tempted to purchase a beautiful stock photo to use for your Pins, but that would be a mistake. Stock photography doesn't yield the best results on Pinterest. Your Pins should be actionable, helpful, and visually compelling. Instead of reaching for a stock image, try out some super fun photo editing tools and get creative. If creativity is not particularly your strong suit, then think about hiring a graphic designer to do the images for you. However you decide to create your images, here is what you should know:

- Faceless images receive about 23 percent more saves that images with faces

- Red and orange Pins perform twice better than blue and multiple-colored Pins

- Pins with less-distracting background gain more traffic

- Simple design works the best

Include Text on Imagery with Overlays

Overlay is another super helpful element that your images should contain. This is great for clarifying the message that your Pin is trying to send as the overlay will improve the readability of the text.

Also, it's good to know that overlays can be quite beneficial when using them in embedded Pins outside of Pinterest (like on your website or blog).

Have Longer Images

When designing your image, make sure to choose 735 px to be the width. As for the length, you can make it as long as you'd like it to be. These longer images can help your content get easily spotted as they tend to really stand out on Pinterest boards.

Keep in mind that it is said that Pins with an aspect ratio of 2:3 or 4:5 receive the most traffic. But if you want to get more click-throughs, then the best hack is to simply include on tall and Pinnable image to be at the top of your blog post.

Determining the Pin Type

Many businesses make the mistake of not using all of the Pin types to their advantage, simply because they are unaware that there are actually more than one type out there. Besides the 'regular' save or repin, there are three more different Pins that you can use in order to increase your reach.

Rich Pins

Rich Pins are standard Pins that you can add some extra context to, in order to give your Pins some more character. These Pins include additional information that the Pinners find super beneficial. They, usually, can be found in 4 categories:

1. Recipe Pins – They attract Pinners with their list of ingredients, cooking times, etc.

2. Product Pins – They make the process of shopping easier thanks to their real-time prices and other product info

3. Article Pins – They show the author name, headlines, description of the story, etc.

4. App Pins – They feature an install button for downloading apps without even leaving Pinterest. This option is only available on iOS.

There are two millions of people who save Rich Pins on a daily basis, so implementing these into your strategy is probably a smart move.

Buyable Pins

Buyable Pins, as the name suggests, are those Pins that have a blue button found next to the red **Pin It** button. They allow Pinners to purchase the product they like, without having to leave Pinterest. How does it work? At this point, all businesses that are on *Shopify* have the opportunity to post Buyable Pins, although they will surely become much more accessible in the near future.

Promoted Pins

Promoted Pins are, in a way, similar to Facebook promotions. You have to buy them in order to reach more followers. These Pins have the ability to increase the rate of engagement from 2 to 5 percent.

There is no minimum cost for these Pins, but the amount that you end up paying depends on your budget and the limit of spending that you set.

At this point, promoted pins are only available to business across the US, Canada, UK, France, Ireland, Australia, and New Zeeland.

Optimize and Engage for Success

Just as with any other social media platform, you will need to optimize your Pins in order to get your pins discovered and saved. It is one thing to make your pin amazing and visually appealing, but if you fail to optimize it for engagement, the beautiful imagery will not do you much good. Here are the ultimate optimization tips for Pinterest that your business should take advantage of:

Pin at the Best Times

If you ask https://www.hubspot.com/, they will tell you that the best time to post on Pinterest is on Saturdays, another platform will tell you that that's Sunday afternoon, but a good rule of a thumb is to save your Pinterest posts for the weeknights and weekends, as you have a lot more chance to be discovered at those times. However, if you want to be more specific, after a lot of research, I've pulled together enough comprehensive data to determine that these are the best times to post on Pinterest:

- Any day at 2-4 a.m., 2-4 p.m., and 8 p.m.-1 a.m.

- Fridays at 3 p.m.

- Saturday Mornings and Saturday Nights from 8 to 11 p.m.

This should work with any time zone, so give them a try and see if they work for your business.

Be Consistent

There are many posts that will suggest pinning up to 10 or even 15 times a day. Other say that once is the key, but the truth is, it is not about pinning a set number of times a day, but about Pinning consistently. If your business can benefit from sharing 20 Pins a day, then by all means, do it. Just keep in mind that if that's your goal, then you should stick to it and provide consistency to your audience. Be consistent so that your followers will know what to expect from your brand.

Make It Easy to be Pinned From

Your content – whether on your website, blog, or your phone app – should be easily Pinnable. If it's not clear to people where they should click in order to pin your content, they will not do it. It's as simple as that. Make sure to download the special widget https://business.pinterest.com/en/pinterest-widget-builder#do_pin_it_button that will add a **'Pin It'** button next to your images, so that people can conveniently Pin from your site.

This actually increases pinning ten times, so do not skip on installing this button.

Pinterest's SEO

Having a decent SEO strategy is more than required, it is essential if you want to attract new Pinners and increase your Saves. When it comes to Pinterest searches, there are only 4 steps of good optimization:

1. Do thorough research on the keywords that are relevant for your business

2. Add those keywords (or keyword phrases) to the titles of your Pins

3. Incorporate the relevant keywords in the Pins' descriptions.

4. Add them to the file names of your Pin images.

For the millionth time, don't go in over your head. Keep in simple and don't use too many keywords. You don't want to be overly selling, but to sound human.

Comment!

It is needless to say but responding to the comments of your followers really goes the extra mile. It shows people that you care about them, that you value their opinion, and that you want to keep them informed and content. Make sure to respond to all of your followers' comments and do it within a day. There is no such thing as "stupid comment". Even if the comment doesn't require a response, such as "Love the color", you should always tell your audience that you value your opinion, at least with "Glad to hear that. Thank you for your feedback".

Commenting is a two-way street. Just like you want your followers to comment on your Pins, you should also leave comments on their boards too. Besides, this will only expose you to a wider audience as their followers will see your comment and your brand as well.

Leveraging Pinterest Marketing in 3 Steps

Even though Pinterest is a platform that is different than the other social media networks, Pinterest Marketing really doesn't require that different approach. When you think about it, it all boils down to just having a clear tactic that will collide with the set business goals you have. To wrap it up, here are the three steps to having a successful Pinterest Marketing campaign:

Step #1: Build Your Brand's Authority

It doesn't matter what you are trying to sell, one of the greatest ways in which you can use Pinterest for your marketing purposes, is to make people become aware of your brand. This is often forgotten as small businesses are usually preoccupied with driving more sales, but what they don't understand is that brand recognition actually results in having more customers.

For instance, if you are in the weight loss niche, you can create a Pinterest board that will promote your products and combine them with other popular weight-loss Pins. That's the beauty of Pinterest, really. Not having to create the entire content yourself but mixing and matching your content with some of the most popular saves on this platform.

Step #2: Grow Your Reach

Although there are many different ways in which you can use Pinterest to grow your reach, one of the most popular techniques is leveraging group boards. The secret here is to team up with some popular Pinners who already have pretty large audiences. By collaborating with them, you get to expose your brand to their audience. Why would they want to do that? Because that way they will provide more value to their loyal fan base.

Just keep in mind that, in order for this joint venture to be successful, you will have to find a partner who has similar interests in order to reach to the right target audience.

Step #3: Drive More Traffic

Without the right traffic, you will never make enough online sales, period. And in order to drive traffic to your website, blog, or even your sales page, you will have to provide your audience with content that is attracting as well as helpful enough to be shared. Pining great visuals is by far the best strategy for driving more traffic, so make sure to use all of the previously mentioned tips and offer your followers content that is inspiring and desirable.

Getting Started with Snapchat

When you think about Social Media Marketing, the first platform that comes to your mind is definitely not Snapchat. However, just because it is not up to par with Facebook, Twitter, and Instagram, it doesn't mean that trying to promote your brand on Snapchat is a wild-goose chase. Quite the opposite.

Snapchat is taking the social world by the storm. It is constantly improving and gaining more users, so missing out on the Snapchatting journey can really be a huge strike for your business. Besides, where the competition is still not that fierce, don't you think that you will be at a slight advantage?

Setting Up the Account

If you are seriously considering giving Snapchat a chance, have in mind that this platform is way different that the ones we've already covered in this book. Here, marketing your brand will not be about using CTAs and links and directing the users to a specific landing page where they can buy your product. Instead, it will be about sharing your brand's story through photos and videos. It may not be a direct way of promoting your products, but it will surely be a great way to spread awareness and tell people know what your business is all about. Here is why businesses choose Snapchat:

- To target a new audience. Snapchat is the go-to platform for teens and millennials and if they happen to be your target audience, then your place is definitely among them.

- Visual sharing. You don't have to brainstorm paragraphs of written content here. The only thing you need to type in is the caption. Everything is visual which is why this platform is so appealing for some businesses.

- Brief posts and stories. Snaps are a 10-second video or a photo. Sharing with your audience will be a pretty quick task, so Snapchatting will not require a lot of your time and effort.

- It all happens in real time. You cannot upload content on Snapchat. It all happens in the spur of the moment.

- Snaps are stories that are deleted after 24 hours (which is mainly the inspiration behind Instagram Stories).

- It has more than 300 million active monthly users, and it is no doubt that introducing your brand on Snapchat will help you increase the brand recognition.

Snapchat is an app created for smartphones only. That means that you can only use Snapchat on your Android or iOS, since it is not available on your desktop or tablet. To set up your Snapchat account and get started, the first thing that you need to do is to download the app. Head to your App Store or the Google Play Store and download the Snapchat app. Then, follow these simple steps:

1. Open the app on your smartphone. Click on **'Sign Up'**.

2. Enter your name and hit **'Sign Up & Accept'**.

3. Next, enter your birthday to verify that you are old enough to be using this app.

4. Choose your username. It has to be at least 3-characters long. Use the name of your business or something that represents it. Tap **'Continue'**.

5. Enter your desired password and click on **'Continue'**.

6. Add your email address.

7. Next, you need to verify your account. Enter your mobile number and you will receive a verification code.

8. Enter the received verification code. Once the code is verified, click on **'Continue'**.

9. Decide whether you want the app to upload your contacts or not.

Now that you've created your account, you will be prompted to take a selfie and add it as a profile picture. After that, click on the white ghost icon in order to select a few photos that best represent your brand.

Snapchat is quite different than the other platforms. In order to know what you are doing, you should have knowledge of its lingo. Here are the most important Snapchat terms you should know of:

Snap – A 10-second video or a photo you take with Snapchat

Story – A photo (or a series) that will last for 24 hours before being deleted

Score – This is the number found below your profile photo and it represents the number of snaps you've viewed and shared.

Chat – Comments with your community

Memories – Published snaps that have a permanent life and cannot disappear after 24 hours (think Instagram Stories Highlights)

Lens – Special effects that are added to the photos

Filter – This is added to the photos in order to commemorate an event

Geofilter – A filter that is added for location-based events

Snapcode – A code (like a QR code) that is used to add friends with a simple button touch

Adding Followers

Taking photos and sharing them on Snapchat will be pointless if you don't have an audience to share your content with. Keep in mind that Snapchat doesn't have a public feed. Your snaps can be seen either by individuals or with everyone who follows your account.

Having a business account, it is of great importance that you add as many people that are relevant to your brand as possible. Seek out followers yourself, don't just wait for people to discover your brand's Snapchat and send you a request.

Use the 'Add Friend' Option – Click on the ghost icon and then tap **'Add Friends'**. You will then see different way in which you can add friends, as well as some recommendations for people you can follow.

Use the Snap Code – By using the snap code, you can easily add friends with a simple button touch. Make sure to encourage people on public events or whatever you get the chance in order to grow your following.

Taking Your Snaps

Congratulations! Your brand is an official Snapchat user. Now that your account is up and running, it is time to learn how to actually take the snaps and share content with your audience:

1. Set your phone so that it faces the subject. For instance, if you are trying to take a snap of your newest product, face your camera away from you and facing the product.

2. Tap the round button to take a photo. To post a video, press this button and hold it for 10 seconds while filming.

3. Add comments to your snaps before you actually publish them:

   Click the T icon for typing text
   Click the pencil icon for writing or drawing text

Click the sticky note to add a sticker – or the scissor icon if you want to create one yourself

4. Click on **'Sent to'**.

5. Decide whether you want to send it to an individual, share with your entire audience, or save it as a *memory*.

6. Finally, click on the **'Save'** button.

Sharing Your Brand's Story

Having your brand present on Snapchat is a great opportunity for increasing awareness. But Snapchat is not like the other social media platforms. Also, if you are a brand, you cannot exactly use Snapchat for posting selfies and sending personal messages as your audience will be uninterested. You have to find a way to present your brand, but without boring those followers who like the selfies and prefer using this platform over the other social media networks.

Here are some ways in which most brands use Snapchat to tell their story. Give these tips a try and craft your own, unique way to share your brand's story with your audience.

Product Launch – Snapchat can actually be the perfect platform for sharing snaps of your newest product to announce a big launch.

Home Tours – If you are in the real estate world, sharing photos or quick videos or available homes on Snapchat can be one great strategy for getting some more offers.

Live Updates – Since Snapchat happens in real time, it is perfect for sharing updates from a live event. Whether a seminar, rock concert, a football match, or a parade, reporting live can be a great way for your brand to attract more viewers.

Product Demo – Have a new product you want to promote? Show your audience how it works or reveal some other hacks that can be done by using it. Short videos are great for this purpose, so don't be afraid to hit the record button.

Behind-the-Scenes Update – IF your audience is impatient for your new line to hit the stores, let them know how hard you are working on it by showing a couple of behind-the-scenes photos. This can be done by showcasing the hard work of your employees or simply by giving a tour of a certain part of your business that your audience doesn't get to see.

Call to Action – Ok, you cannot use CTAs like with other social media platforms, but you can surely create some snaps that can encourage your followers to take an action, whether it is to sign up or go to an online (or physical) store and make a purchase.

Guest Introduction – Want to introduce your guest for your next Twitter Chat, podcast, or your YouTube show? Snapchat can help you make the announcement in a few visual snaps.

Coupons – Did you know that businesses actually use the doodle feature on Snapchat in order to share discounts and promotional codes? Why not give this a try and see how this works for your business?

Target Specific Users – Do you think that you have some followers that can benefit from purchasing your products or services the most? Why not approach them directly via private messages and make them an offer? For instance, if you are an owner of a massage studio and you notice a stay-at-home mom of 4, you can send a private message to her admiring her patience and hard work, and offering her a huge discount for a massage treatment or even a free massage? This may not only make her a paying customer in the future, but she will most likely end up recommending your business to her circle of friends.

Engage!

While sharing snaps on Snapchat is a great way to increase brand recognition, gain more followers, and keep the ones you have informed and entertained, Snapchat is not a one-way street. Making sure to encourage engagement on Snapchat is just as interacting with your followers matter on the other social media platforms.

When you swipe the bottom of a user's snap, you will see that there is a *Send a Chat* where people can write down your comments. That means that on every snap you post, your followers have the opportunity to engage with the content and ask questions. And I am not only asking for the price of the newest products or asking if that silk shirt comes in different colors. I am talking about making sure that each of your snaps is thoughtful and created with the purpose to keep your audience engaged.

Here are some tips on encouraging interaction from your community, that most Snapchatting businesses use in order to increase the rate of engagement:

Share Content that Requires a Response – Although this is probably easier to achieve on other social media platforms, posting content that requires a response on Snapchat is indeed possible. But just because you have no clue on how to achieve this doesn't mean that you shouldn't do it. Have your whole team involved and let each of them share with you what makes them respond to content. Pull out the best thoughts together and come up with the best strategy that works for your brand.

Ask Open-Ended Questions – It is a bit more challenging, but asking questions on Snapchat is surely possible. Want to draw the attention of your users? Take a snap and press 'T' to type in the question. Just make sure that your questions deserve a bit more than a simple yes or no to keep the conversation alive.

Encourage to Respond with a Snap – Ok, let's be honest. Snapchat is a visual app and people go there to take snaps and look at other people's images. Your audience will be probably more interested in responding to you with a snap than with a text, so make sure to give them the opportunity.

Be Creative and Ask Different Responses – Let your followers respond with stickers, doodles or a special filter. Let them get even more creative and ask them to actually make their own filter.

Be Humorous – Keep in mind that your audience is on Snapchat for light-hearted and fun content. They are not looking for deep and meaningful conversation, so make sure to turn on your humorous side in your posts.

Create a Contest – People love challenges and competitions. By creating one, you will not only get your audience thrilled to participate, but you will also get to make the lucky winner a happy person. For instance, have a competition where your followers should use your brand name in a fun sentence, or take a funny snap with your product, or show you a snap of your product doing something that is not its main purpose. The point is for people to get engaged with your brand. Announce a huge reward for the funniest person. For instance, a special membership, a really generous discount on an expensive line, free products or services, etc. This can help you spread brand awareness, increase the engagement rate, and ultimately drive more sales.

Respond to Every Snap and Comment – Just like wit every other social media platform, responding to every question, snap, or feedback – whether positive or not – can have a great impact on your relationship with your audience. Respond in kind and let your followers know that you appreciate when someone takes the time to reach out.

Reward People Who Reach Out with Snaps – If you want to further motivate your audience to engage with your brand, you should be ready to give them something in return. This is especially important for small businesses who don't have an established fan base just yet. By rewarding your audience, you get to promote your brand, spread recognition, and keep your followers interested in what you are offering as well. Let your customers know that for every shared snap they will be getting a 10 or 20 percent discount on a certain product or service.

Snapchat may not seem like the go-to platform for marketing your brand, but it definitely has valuable marketing opportunities to offer. By taking on the challenge to promote your business in this unique way, you show your audience another side of you that they cannot see on, let's say, Twitter.